~STALKING THE RED HEADED STRANGER~

ALSO BY RANDY POE

Music Publishing: A Songwriter's Guide

Squeeze My Lemon: A Collection of Classic Blues Lyrics

The New Songwriter's Guide to Music Publishing

Skydog: The Duane Allman Story

~STALKING THE RED HEADED STRANGER~

or

HOW TO GET YOUR SONGS INTO THE HANDS
OF THE ARTISTS WHO REALLY MATTER

Through

SHOW BUSINESS TRICKERY,
UNDERHANDED SKULLDUGGERY,
SHREWDNESS, AND CHICANERY

As Well As

VARIOUS LESS NEFARIOUS METHODS OF SONG PLUGGING

★ ★ ★ ★ ★

A PRACTICAL HANDBOOK
AND HISTORICAL PORTRAIT

~ RANDY POE ~

Hal Leonard Books
An Imprint of Hal Leonard Corporation

Published in 2012 by Hal Leonard Books
An Imprint of Hal Leonard Corporation
7777 West Bluemound Road
Milwaukee, WI 53213

Trade Book Division Editorial Offices
33 Plymouth St., Montclair, NJ 07042

"The Girls I Never Kissed" (Jerry Leiber/Mike Stoller) © 1972, 1986 Jerome Leiber Music/Purple Starfish Music. All rights administered by Sony/ATV Music Publishing LLC, 8 Music Square West, Nashville, TN 37203. All rights reserved. Used by permission.

Photos on pages 4 and 98 courtesy of the Leiber & Stoller Archives. Photos on page 21, 85, 87, and 90 from the Sam Teicher Collection, courtesy of the Songwriters Hall of Fame Archives. Photos on pages 47, 52, 110, and 115 from Shutterstock. Photo on page 78 © Bettmann/Corbis. Photo on page 72 courtesy of Sam Teicher. Photo on page 204 courtesy of Getty/WireImage. Photo on page 63 from Photofest. Photos on pages 169, 223, 228, 230, and 253 by Randy Poe. All other photos are from the author's collection.

Printed in the United States of America

Book design by Damien Castaneda

Library of Congress Cataloging-in-Publication Data

Poe, Randy, 1955-
  Stalking the red headed stranger, or, How to get your songs into the hands of the artists who really matter through show business trickery, underhanded skullduggery, shrewdness, and chicanery as well as various less nefarious methods of song plugging / Randy Poe.
     p. cm.
  ISBN 978-1-4584-0274-5 (pbk.)
  1. Music trade--Vocational guidance. 2. Popular music--Writing and publishing. I. Title. II. Title: Stalking the red headed stranger. III. Title: How to get your songs into the hands of the artists who really matter through show business trickery, underhanded skullduggery, shrewdness, and chicanery as well as various less nefarious methods of song plugging.
  ML3790.P64 2012
  781.64023--dc23
                            2011052638

www.halleonardbooks.com

"There are no bad days"

—Randall "Poodie" Locke, 1948–2009

A NOTE FROM THE AUTHOR

I finished writing *Stalking the Red Headed Stranger* in the wee, small hours of Sunday morning, August 21, 2011. Less than twenty-four hours later, Jerry Leiber passed away at the age of seventy-eight.

As you will read in the pages ahead, Jerry Leiber is a very important part of this story, just as he has been a very important part of my life for more than a quarter century.

As I sit at this keyboard trying to envision a world without Jerry, my mind drifts back to a business meeting at Leiber and Stoller's publishing headquarters several years ago. Mike Stoller's son Peter and I were sitting with the two songwriters, excitedly expressing our latest ideas on how best to promote what we kept referring to as "the legacy of Leiber and Stoller." Peter and I had used the word "legacy" about a half dozen times, when Jerry slowly raised his left hand to silence us. After one of his perfectly timed dramatic pauses, he looked me right in the eye and said, "Don't say 'legacy.' Please. Say, '*living* legacy.'"

Jerry Leiber—the consummate word man.

And so, for this book, the living legacy remains, and the tense shall not be past. If there's one thing of which I am absolutely certain, it is this: the songs of Leiber and Stoller will outlive us all.

To quote one of Jerry Leiber's most famous lyrics, "Let's break out the booze and have a ball." I hope you enjoy this book as much as I enjoyed writing it for you.

August 23, 2011

INTRODUCTION

One day in 1969, Johnny Cash and his wife, June Carter, were sitting in their house in Hendersonville, Tennessee, when a helicopter landed on their lawn. The pilot was a young songwriter named Kris Kristofferson. Kristofferson stepped out of the chopper with a beer in one hand and a cassette tape of "Sunday Morning Coming Down" in the other.

★ ★ ★ ★ ★

I saw Johnny Cash perform "Sunday Morning Coming Down" on TV one night and listened as he told the story: "Here's a song written by my friend Kris Kristofferson, and I got it in a very strange way," Cash said. "I got it right out of the sky. One afternoon, June said, 'Some fool has landed in our yard in a helicopter.' Here was Kris, and he said, 'I thought this might be the best way to get a song to you—bring it right out of the sky.' I said, 'You got it. Let's listen to it.'"

Johnny Cash's recording of "Sunday Morning Coming Down" hit the country charts in September of 1970, eventually reaching No. 1. The record even made the Top 50 on the pop charts, and went on to receive the Country Music Association's award for "Song of the Year."

I've heard a lot of great song plugging anecdotes during my thirty-plus years in the music business, and the one about Kris Kristofferson pitching "Sunday Morn-

Kristofferson's first album included his own version of "Sunday Morning Coming Down," as well as a song that would become a posthumous hit for Janis Joplin. After Janis's record hit the top of the pop charts, Kris's debut album was given a new cover photo and a new title: *Me and Bobby McGee.*

ing Coming Down" to Johnny Cash via helicopter is among my all-time favorites. And of course, hardly a word of the tale is true.

Johnny Cash had "a very creative memory," says Kris. The songwriter did, indeed, land a helicopter on Johnny Cash's lawn once—but as Kris recalls the events of that day, Cash wasn't even at home. And the tape Kristofferson had with him that he wanted to give to the absentee Cash was actually "a song nobody ever cut" called "It No Longer Matters." As far as the beer in one hand and cassette in the other is concerned, Kris points out, "If I'd ever tried to fly a helicopter with a beer, I don't know where the hell I'd put it, because you've got to use both hands to fly!" Luckily, Johnny Cash wasn't one to let the truth get in the way of a good song plugging story.

Back in a previous millennium, I wrote my first book—*Music Publishing: A Songwriter's Guide*—which explained how the semi-mysterious business of music publishing works. Even though I'm a music publisher myself, I'm first and foremost a lover of songs and a fan of songwriters, so I wrote the music publishing book in an attempt to create a more level playing field for those wanting to get their songs published without getting ripped off too badly in the process. In those pages, I covered practically everything I knew about the subject of music publishing except song plugging. I provided a definition of song plugging in its simplest form (matching a song with an artist and then attempting to get that artist to record the song in question), but I didn't go into much detail about the history of song plugging or how songs are pitched. Why not? Because I figured it would take another entire book to try to cover the subject properly. Turns out I was right.

In truth, there isn't any one specific way to plug a song any more than there's one specific way to sell a used car, pitch a script to a motion picture studio, or convince your kids to brush their teeth. In the end, it's about strategy and salesmanship. And you can't possibly make the sale unless you first devise a successful plan for familiarizing the potential buyer with what you're selling—be it a song, a car, a script, or the concept of cavity-free teeth.

I once saw a television commercial promoting a medical treatment center. Throughout the TV ad, there was some tiny type running across the bottom of the screen. Eventually curiosity got the best of me, so I rolled off of my sofa and got about six inches away from my television set. After no small amount of effort and squinting, I could finally read the phrase scrolling across the screen: "No cases are typical." Now I had seen ads in the past with the disclaimer "Not all cases are typical," but a disclaimer that absolutely no cases were typical didn't strike me as being the greatest sales pitch in the world (which probably explains why the type was so tiny). But as phrases go, it's a perfect description of song plugging.

In the traditional definition of the term, song plugging begins with determining the right performer for a particular song and then determining a way to get that recording artist to hear that song. At that point—barring coercion, bribery, or blackmail (none of which needs to be entirely ruled out)—the decision to actually record the song is in the hands of the artist, or the artist's producer, or the artist's girlfriend and/or the artist's boyfriend, or a record label executive, or the artist's psychic, or any number of other people. Or sometimes it's a matter of just plain old luck. (Producer: "We have another half hour of studio time and we're out of songs. Got any ideas?" Artist: "I think there's a demo out in the trunk of my car. Let's give it a listen and see if it's any good.")

★ ★ ★ ★ ★

When I told some of my LA-based music-business cohorts that I was going to write a book about song plugging, the response I got from just about everyone was the same: "Why would you want to do that? Song plugging is a lost art. It doesn't exist anymore." I thanked each and every one of them for their moral support, and then politely explained that my definition of song plugging is a bit broader than the conventional definition of the term.

Back before the Beatles came along and rewrote the music business by writing their own songs, the song plugger was a vital part of every music publishing company. The iconic singers of the pre–rock & roll era—Frank Sinatra, Tony Bennett, Nat "King" Cole, Johnny Mathis, Dean Martin, Rosemary Clooney, Ella Fitzgerald, Andy Williams, Doris Day, and a bunch of other performers your great-grandparents listened to—were in constant need of new songs. Those works had to be written by men and women whose sole job was songwriting. And once they were written, it was the song plugger's job to take those songs and try to get Sinatra and the rest to record them. Today that kind of song plugger is rare, except in Nashville where there is still a large community of songwriters whose sole job is to write great country songs. The Nashville music publishing community is rife with song pluggers, and it will stay that way unless the day comes that all country artists decide to perform only songs they write themselves.

In addition to many country artists, there are still plenty of pop singers who also choose to record songs written by others. Nobody (in their right mind) tries to pitch songs to singers or bands that write all their own songs. If you think you've written a great song that would be perfect for one of those acts, you might want to rejoin the rest of us here in the real world and focus your songwriting energies on artists who still—at least occasionally—rely on outside material to record.

The world of song plugging doesn't revolve solely around pop and country music. I've pitched tunes to blues artists, R&B acts, cabaret singers, bluegrass groups, and performers from various other genres. It's all about matching the right song with the right singer.

But my definition of song plugging goes beyond the act of trying to get an artist to record a song. Song plugging can also include pitching songs to be used in movies, TV shows, commercials, video games, or other formats in need of music. When karaoke first arrived in the US, I dove into that world before most people in music publishing even knew how to pronounce it. Granted, it helped that I was representing a huge collection of classic rock & roll songs at the time, but the point is this: If you have a song that you are actively trying to promote, it doesn't matter what your official job title is or if you have no title at all. You're still a song plugger.

★ ★ ★ ★ ★

Matching a song with an artist and then getting the artist to hear that song sounds pretty simple. And sometimes it can be—except, perhaps, when you have a boss who says he wants you to track down one of the most famous people on the planet and play a song for him "face-to-face"—especially if you're based in Los Angeles and the American icon he wants you to play it for is on a tour bus rapidly heading across Canada from west to east. It also doesn't help if that famous artist has no clue who you are, or that you're heading his way, or *why* you're heading his way, or that you have an appointment with him—especially if you don't.

This is a book about song plugging, how and why it began; how some major hits of the past came about through the efforts of song pluggers; how to pitch your own songs, or songs you represent; and how I got into the music business and became a song plugger (among other things), including the incredible—but absolutely true—story of how I once traveled over 8,000 miles by plane, taxi, rental car, and ferryboat to pitch a single song to Willie Nelson.

~STALKING THE RED HEADED STRANGER~

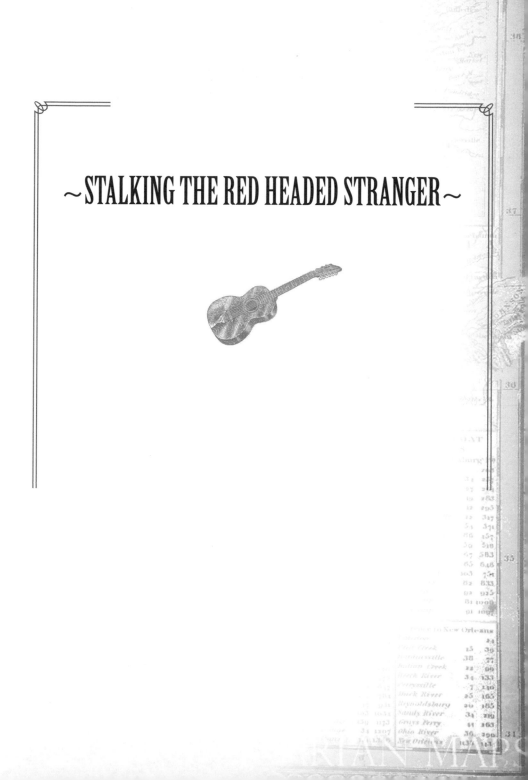

CHAPTER ONE

★ ☆ ★

Anybody trying to survive in the music business is lucky to hang on to the same job for more than a few years. It seems that every December—while most folks are getting ready to celebrate the holidays—record labels, music publishing companies, booking agencies, management firms, and concert-promotion conglomerates are busy announcing their annual list of layoffs. Somehow, there are always plenty of people left to keep all those companies afloat. (I have this theory that every time a new CEO is brought in to run a major record label or multinational music publishing company, he or she overhires like crazy, just so there'll be people to let go in December.)

Some of those who get fired at year's end find jobs at other companies; some of the more entrepreneurial-minded form new companies; some become "consultants" (the much-used music business term that means "I've recently been fired and haven't found another job yet"); and some of those who managed to keep from getting fired in the first place decide to move from one music company to another anyway—because they think they might be getting fired soon, or because they don't like where they're working, or because they feel it's the best way to move on up the music-industry ladder.

I appear to be the exception that proves the rule, because I've remained at the same job since the mid-1980s. Nobody is supposed to stay at the same company in the music business for over a quarter century, but as I write these words, I've done just that.

I'm the president of Leiber & Stoller Music Publishing in Los Angeles. The owners of the company are Jerry Leiber and Mike Stoller, two of the most successful songwriters of all time. They wrote "Hound Dog," "Jailhouse Rock," and over twenty other songs recorded by Elvis Presley. And then there's "Kansas City," "Love Potion # 9," "Yakety Yak," "Charlie Brown," and "I'm a Woman." They also cowrote "Stand By Me" with Ben E. King and "On Broadway" with Barry Mann and Cynthia Weil. Their theatrical show, *Smokey Joe's Café: The Songs of Leiber & Stoller*, holds the record for being the longest running musical revue in Broadway history. They've been inducted into both the rock & roll Hall of Fame and the Songwriters Hall of Fame.*

Not only have the works of Leiber and Stoller made well over 100 appearances on the Billboard charts, their songs continue to be recorded and performed all over the world today. Numerous recordings of their songs, many of which they also produced, have been sampled by some of today's biggest-selling rap and hip-hop artists.

(L-R) Mike Stoller, Elvis Presley, and Jerry Leiber at MGM Studios (1957).

----

* The colorful and compelling chronicle of the lives and careers of Jerry Leiber and Mike Stoller is told in the two songwriters' own words in their critically acclaimed book, *Hound Dog: The Leiber & Stoller Autobiography*. *Hound Dog* is filled with great stories from these two masters of songwriting who not only changed the course of popular music, but who were also responsible for major changes within the music business itself.

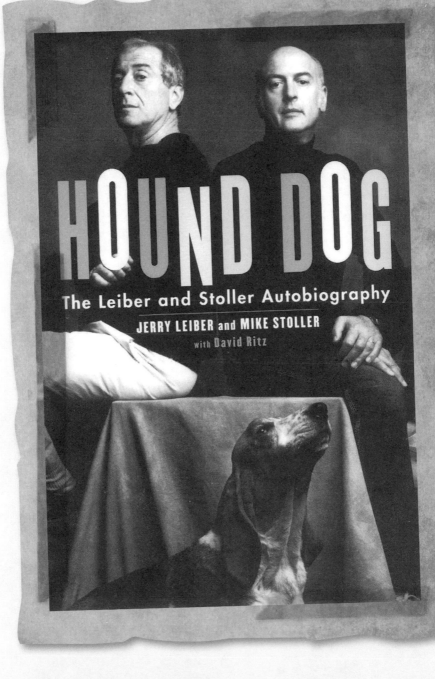

HOUND DOG

The Leiber and Stoller Autobiography

JERRY LEIBER and MIKE STOLLER
with David Ritz

In addition to the aforementioned Elvis Presley and Ben E. King, among the over 1,000 acts that have recorded songs written by Leiber and Stoller are the Beatles, the Rolling Stones, the Grateful Dead, B. B. King, James Brown, Little Richard, Jerry Lee Lewis, the Beach Boys, Buddy Holly, Fats Domino, Jimi Hendrix, ZZ Top, Buck Owens, Muddy Waters, Tom Jones, George Jones, Norah Jones, Count Basie, Eric Clapton, Neil Diamond, Liza Minnelli, Bobby Darin, John Mellencamp, Neil Young, Aretha Franklin, Peggy Lee, Johnny Cash, Dwight Yoakam, Trisha Yearwood, the Coasters, the Drifters, the Monkees, Queen, David Bowie, Tom Petty and the Heartbreakers, Little Feat, Ray Charles, Barbra Streisand, James Taylor, Bette Midler, Reba McEntire, Tony Bennett, and Frank Sinatra.

And speaking of Frank Sinatra . . .

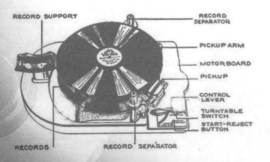

CHAPTER TWO

One day I got a call from Jerry Leiber, asking me to come to his house to go over some paperwork with him. Jerry's incredible house is right on the beach, so I always look forward to his phone calls inviting me out to his place. I get to escape from the office, I get to slip in a quick stroll on the beach, and I

Stardust—Nelson's album of pop standards would remain on the charts for over a decade and sell more than 5,000,000 copies.

get to hang out with one of the greatest lyricists of all time in one of the most gorgeous oceanfront houses in town. What could be better than that?

We were both sitting at Jerry's dining room table going over various documents that had accumulated since the last time I'd been to see him, when he suddenly looked up from the paperwork and said, "Hey man, I just came up with a killer idea for the Sinatra Song!"

The Sinatra Song is a Leiber and Stoller composition called "The Girls I Never Kissed," recorded by Frank Sinatra in 1986. It's the sole song written by Jerry and Mike that neither of them ever refers to by its actual title. The Beatles recorded a half dozen Leiber and Stoller songs. Peggy Lee recorded a dozen and a half. Elvis recorded almost two dozen. The Coasters recorded close to 100. But since Ol' Blue Eyes recorded only one, both Leiber and Stoller refer to "The Girls I Never Kissed" simply as "the Sinatra Song."

"You know the Sinatra Song, right?" Jerry asked. Before I could answer, he said, "Well, what I want you to do is hand deliver it to your buddy Willie."

I knew the Sinatra Song all right, but I couldn't think of any buddies of mine named Willie, nor why he would need the Sinatra Song hand-delivered to him.

"Yes, I'm very familiar with the Sinatra Song," I said. "It's got a beautiful melody, and the subject of the lyrics require that it be sung by an older man, which is why it was so perfect for Sinatra."

"Well, Willie Nelson's the same age I am—which ain't young—so give him a call and let him know you want to bring it to him."

I sat there dumbfounded. "Willie *Nelson*?"

"What's the matter? You don't think he could sing it? He did that *Stardust* album and it sold millions of copies. He's not just a country artist. He can sing standards, and the Sinatra Song is one of the few things Mike and I have written that has a real shot at becoming a standard someday." He paused for a moment and then added, "Oh, maybe you don't think it's right for him."

I've always been amazed that a songwriter of Jerry Leiber's stature values my opinion when it comes to matching songs with artists. I've also found it fascinating that he doesn't realize most of us would consider practically all of the hits he and Mike Stoller have written to be standards. But I understood what he meant: to Jerry's way of thinking, Irving Berlin, Cole Porter, Rodgers and Hammerstein—the writers of his youth—wrote virtually all of the standards already. As he and Mike have said in many interviews, they thought the R&B and rock & roll hits they were writing in the 1950s and 1960s were like the Sunday comics—something that could entertain you briefly, but would soon be forgotten. Neither of the writers could imagine their songs would remain popular for well over half a century—or that they'd end up with forty of those songs in a Broadway show that would garner seven Tony nominations and a Grammy Award for its cast album.

~ THE MATCH GAME ~

One of the essential keys to song plugging is to be able to match the right song with the right artist. Willie Nelson once wrote a song called "The Words Don't Fit the Picture." One glance at the title and you know exactly what the song is going to be about—two lovers who turn out not to be the right match for each other.

When it comes to song plugging, the song you want to pitch has to be the right match for a specific artist. It's a simple concept, but the trick is to have "ears," and to be as familiar with an artist as possible before you send a song to their record producer, manager, etc. Listen to his or her current hit or latest album. Check out his or her videos online. Too many times I've heard, "I'm sure [Major Country Act] could sing this song." No doubt that's true. The great ones can sing a page from the phonebook and bring you to tears—but odds are they're not interested in warbling about the collected Niedermeyers of Goobertown, Arizona. They want to sing a song that fits their style and vocal range. And of course, they want to have "hit" written all over it.

Always do your research first. If you manage to get your song heard by the right people in a specific artist's camp, the last thing you want is to end up being stuck with the reputation of not knowing how to play the match game.

When Jerry suggested that I might not think the song was right for Willie, he gave me the opening I needed to confess that Willie Nelson and I were not buddies. We weren't even acquaintances. I'd only been in the same room with the man a few times in my life, and all but one of those times was very brief. I'd also actually been on his tour bus once, but I'd spent the whole time talking to Willie's sister and one of his guitar players while Willie was conversing with a friend of mine (my friend being the only reason I was on the bus in the first place). I couldn't imagine why Jerry thought Willie and I were friends, but my ego got the best of me, and I passed up the opportunity to admit that Willie Nelson wouldn't know Randy Poe from Edgar Allan Poe.

"Of course the Sinatra Song's right for him," I said. "I'm sure he could kill it."

"Great! Then I want you to call him, get on a plane, and take it to him. I want you to sit with him, face-to-face, and play him the Sinatra Song. Willie's recorded all those standards throughout his career, so I'll bet he's a huge Frank Sinatra fan."

"Okay," I said. "You got it."

"Where does he live? Nashville?"

"No, he lives near Austin, Texas—and he's got a place on Maui," I said, exhausting my Willie Nelson real estate trivia knowledge in a single sentence while unwisely reinforcing the idea that we were pals.

"Then call him up, find out which house he's at this week, and book a flight. If he cuts the tune, I'll buy you a green tie"—no doubt the first time anyone has ever made reference to Willie Nelson and Oscar Wilde in the same sentence.

At that moment, Jerry's next appointment arrived, giving me the chance to make a quick getaway. It's difficult to kick oneself and drive at the same time, but I was doing a pretty good job of it as I headed back to the office. Why hadn't I just admitted that Willie Nelson and I weren't pals? How enormous could my ego possibly be? I didn't have an answer for that one (although I'm sure most of my friends, family members, and coworkers would have been happy to fill me in).

CHAPTER THREE

O n the way back to my office on Sunset Boulevard, I thought about how Leiber and Stoller had uniquely solved the whole song plug-ging dilemma early on in their careers by becoming label owners and record producers. In 1954, when they had both reached the ripe old age of twenty-one, they formed Spark Records in Los Angeles, as

Leiber & Stoller Present the Spark Records Story – A compilation album featuring 30 tracks from the Spark label, including the Robins's "Smokey Joe's Café."

~THE PRODUCER~

The first rule regarding who selects the songs for a recording session is this: "There are no rules." Outside the obvious desire of all involved that every song on the CD should have the potential to be a hit, the actual parties who choose the songs for that CD can be diverse and numerous. However, as a general rule, if any one person is in charge, it's usually the record producer.

Back in Leiber and Stoller's heyday, if they were in the studio, they were usually producing recordings of songs they had written themselves. A record producer who is also a hit songwriter is a recording artist's best friend (and a song plugger's worst nightmare).

Luckily, most producers' talents lie in creating the right sound and atmosphere for a record, and the songwriting is frequently left up to others (although the savvy producer will usually try to squeeze in a song or two of his own). If you can't get your song directly to the artist, that artist's record producer is frequently your next best choice. In addition, one of the assets of having access to a successful record producer is that he or she most likely produces multiple artists. Even if artist A doesn't want to record a song you've pitched to that artist's record producer, it might be an even better fit for artist B—the very artist B whom the producer will be in the studio with next week. And hey, if that extremely important record producer wants to contribute a word change here or a chord change there and become a cowriter of the song you're pitching, you might want to consider this other important music business rule: "It's better to have 50 percent of something than 100 percent of nothing."

well as their own music publishing company. In many cases they would write four songs, take one of their label's acts into the recording studio, and cut all four songs in three hours. While most song pluggers might spend weeks trying to charm an artist into merely listening to a single song, Leiber and Stoller were in a recording studio averaging one new cut every forty-five minutes. Absolutely brilliant.

Of course, it helped that they had a knack for writing great songs for specific artists—songs that were strong both lyrically and melodically with a commercial quality that appealed to post–World War II record-buying teens.

One of those songs on Spark was "Smokey Joe's Café," recorded by a vocal group called the Robins. The record caught the ears of the top executives at Atlantic Records in New York City, which soon led to Atlantic leasing the master of "Smokey Joe's Café" from Leiber and Stoller and rereleasing it on Atlantic's subsidiary label, Atco, where it became a Top 10 hit on the R&B charts.

Excited by the success of "Smokey Joe's Café," as well as the extraordinary talents of these two young men just barely out of their teens, Atlantic's Ahmet Ertegun and Jerry Wexler encouraged Leiber and Stoller to move to New York and work for the label, becoming in-house producers for a weekly salary. L&S—having worked only for themselves from the beginning of their songwriting/ record-producing careers—passed on the offer, but agreed to move to New York and produce records for Atlantic and other record labels in exchange for a production royalty to be paid on every record sold. It was a concept no one had ever thought of before, making Leiber and Stoller the first independent record producers in the business. Absolutely brilliant again.

CHAPTER FOUR

Usually the president of a very large independent music publishing company doesn't include song plugging as part of his job description. But in 2003—after spending years building up their music publishing assets by signing writers and acquiring various other independent publishing companies—Leiber and Stoller sold all of the copyrights they owned except for the songs the two of them had written (and a hand-selected few written by others). This, of course, resulted in substantial downsizing, and that downsizing caused those of us who remained at the company to have to pitch in (pardon the pun) in certain areas that had previously been handled by others.

Until the sale in 2003, I had spent many years sitting in my fancy office, telling everybody else who worked there what to do. Every now and then, I would get a call from a record producer, a manager, or a friend of an artist, letting me know that so-and-so was in the studio and asking me for song suggestions. I would throw out ideas to the caller, sometimes ending up with songs on the record and sometimes not. I also included songs from our publishing company on CDs that I compiled for various record labels. But for the most part, I was no longer what anyone would consider a hyperactive song plugger. I had an independent song plugger in Nashville. I also had people on staff in LA who pitched songs to artists as well as to music supervisors in an effort to get works from our publishing company used in movies and TV shows. In truth, other folks were doing almost all of the song plugging, so my job was to let them do their jobs. But by the time Jerry Leiber told me to go play the Sinatra Song for Willie Nelson, there was hardly anyone else left at the company to pitch songs to artists.

Of course, anyone who has ever worked at a company that has substantially downsized is very aware that the workload can become pretty intense for those who have been lucky enough to keep their jobs. And so, in the process of working ten hours or more a day, I managed to completely forget all about Jerry's orders to take the Sinatra Song to Willie Nelson. Hey, it happens.

CHAPTER FIVE

★ ✬ ★

About three weeks after my visit to Jerry's house, I was sitting in my office when the receptionist told me Mike was on the phone and needed to talk to me. I grabbed the receiver and said, "Hi Mike. What's up?"

"Well," he said, "I just got off the phone with Jerry. I'm calling to tell you he's not very happy with you."

"Uh oh. What did I do?"

"Actually, it's what you didn't do. He says he told you to take the Sinatra Song to Willie Nelson and you didn't do it."

In that instant, the queasiness I'd been feeling three weeks earlier at Jerry's house came rushing back. "Oh man, I completely forgot," I confessed.

"I'm just giving you the message, but my advice would be to follow through with what he told you to do."

"Of course," I said. "By the way, Willie Nelson tours constantly. I don't even know where he is right now."

"I'd strongly recommend that you find out."

"Okay. I'm on it." He hung up the phone, leaving me to begin playing a new game of my own invention called "Where's Willie?"

My eyes moved from the telephone to the wall on my left, filled with gold and platinum records; to the wall to my right, covered with more gold and platinum records; and then to the wall directly in front of me: my "Wall of Fame"—a collection of photos of yours truly posing with various famous folks, taken over the years at assorted awards dinners and other music industry functions. Among them were Michael Jackson, B. B. King, Priscilla

~ WRITE IT DOWN! ~

Years ago I worked in the same office with an older gentleman who was an incessant list maker. He always kept a stack of yellow legal pads on his desk that he filled with lists of calls he had received, calls he had to return, things he had to do that day, that week, that month . . . I had never known anyone who kept such copious work notes. Since I was about half his age, I chalked it up to the failing memory of an old man. Now that I'm older than he was then, I realize that man was a genius.

Unless you're one of the few people on the planet who has eidetic memory— also known as "total recall"—you're likely to forget things from time to time. Let me assure you, memory isn't something that improves with age.

As a song plugger, you need to keep track of every pitch you make. Nothing is more embarrassing than to be sitting in a listening session with a record producer, only to have him say, "As you might recall, I didn't like this song the last time you played it for me."

Keep a log of your songs, a list of the parties you've pitched them to, a list of potential parties to pitch specific songs to in the future, a list of those who've turned certain songs down, a list of those who are currently holding specific songs for future consideration, a list of songs that have been recorded but not yet released, a list of songs you've pitched to music supervisors for potential film uses, as well as any other notes you need to keep—because nobody can remember everything.

Here's a rule to live by: if you can remember everything you've ever pitched and the current status of each of those pitches, you're not working hard enough.

Unlike my old coworker, you don't have to kill trees anymore. You can keep track of everything using Excel spreadsheets or any other software program that works for you.

Even when you use your best efforts, every once in a while you'll probably still find yourself having to say, "Oh man, I completely forgot." The more you write things down, the fewer times you'll have to confess forgetfulness. Having been there a few times myself, I can promise it's better to make lists and have someone think you have a bad memory than to keep no lists at all and prove that they're right.

Presley, Chuck Berry, Jerry Lee Lewis, Henry Mancini, Neil Diamond, Brian Wilson, Tony Bennett, Willie Nelson . . . Willie Nelson? Uh oh.

There were actually *three* Willie photos on the Wall of Fame. One was of Willie and me at a Songwriters Hall of Fame dinner in 1983. (At the time it was taken, I was executive director of the National Academy of Popular Music/Songwriters Hall of Fame. Willie was getting a lifetime achievement award from the Academy that year, and it was my job to make sure everything went as smoothly as possible. That night, as I was leading Willie from the lobby of the Waldorf Astoria into the section of the hotel where the event was to take place, the Hall of

Fame's staff photographer had taken a picture of the two of us together.)

Next to the Songwriters Hall of Fame photo was a publicity photo of Willie that read, "To Randy Poe, Thanks, Willie Nelson, '93." (My best friend, Roger Deitz, who knew I was a huge fan of the singer, had been on the tour bus with Willie after a concert and had asked the singer to autograph a photo to me.)

Next to the autographed publicity photo was a picture of Willie and me taken at Ray Charles's seventieth birthday party at the House of Blues in Los Angeles in 2000. (I was a friend of the PR person handling the event—as were Leiber and Stoller—so I ended up in the "Green Room," where absolutely everyone was getting their picture taken with Willie.)

As I stared at the photos in front of me, I literally saw the handwriting on the wall. No wonder Jerry Leiber thought Willie and I were good buddies. According to the photos—the very photos Jerry had seen every time he'd walked into my office—Willie and I had been hanging out together since the early 1980s!

By 2006, in the more than two decades that I'd worked for Leiber and Stoller, I'd never failed to accomplish any task they'd assigned to me—and be-

Photos from my "Wall of Fame"— With Chuck Berry...

lieve me, on a few occasions they'd asked me to do the near impossible. As Willie smiled downed at me from the wall, I realized I had no option—absolutely no alternative. I decided, then and there, that I would discover the whereabouts of Willie Nelson, that I would make contact with Willie Nelson, and that I would do what Jerry had told me to do: "Sit with him, face-to-face, and play him the Sinatra Song."

...and Michael Jackson.

CHAPTER SIX

★ ✹ ★

These days, pitching a song is actually a pretty easy task compared to the song pluggers' job in the early days of music publishing. Before iTunes, before CDs, before vinyl albums and singles—even before 78-rpm records, cylinder recordings, and piano rolls—there were song pluggers. The job title has been around for well over 100 years, but the actual duties of the song plugger have changed dramatically.

In the late 1800s, pluggers were employed by music publishing companies to promote the companies' sheet music. In those years, the number of copies of sheet music of a specific song sold by a music publisher was the sole way of determining whether or not a song was a "hit."

There's so much noise in our lives and technology at our fingertips in the twenty-first century that it's pretty hard to imagine what the late nineteenth century home must have been like: No sound coming from a television set, no music wafting from a radio or blasting from a stereo, no iTunes playing through computer speakers, no video games . . . Houses belonging to Americans prior to the mass production of cylinder recordings, gramophone discs, and radios were generally filled with silence.

It was an era when you had to be proactive if you wanted the sound of musical entertainment in your home. You needed at least one instrument in the parlor and at least one person in the family who could play it.

For most nineteenth-century Americans, the musical instrument of choice was the piano. And if someone in the family learned to read music, sheet music would be purchased so the family could stand around the piano and sing, while the pianist in the family read and played the musical notes transcribed on that sheet music.

Music publishers stayed in business, then, by printing sheet music and selling it to all those people with pianos in their parlors. The goal of each music publisher was to convince those piano-owning families to want to buy the sheet music of the songs the publisher printed. Thus the position of the song plugger was created.

"Song plugger" is definitely an odd job title, but perhaps it sounds slightly more impressive than "traveling salesman," which is essentially what song pluggers of that era were. Music publishers hired song pluggers to go around the country selling sheet music to a town's music stores, department stores, and the local "five and dimes." (In case you're too young to remember them—and unless you're even older than I am, you'd just about have to be—"five and dimes" were variety stores that carried items that cost either five or ten cents.)

Unlike their modern-day equivalent, song pluggers of the late 1800s and early 1900s had to be able to sing and play the piano. It was the plugger's job to "sell" the song by performing it. If the person in charge of deciding what sheet music was going to be sold in the store liked the song the plugger was plugging, he or she would order copies of the sheet music of that particular song.

At that point, the song plugger's job was done for the day, and he would take his wares on to the next town. Meanwhile, the stores that bought the sheet music also had a person on staff with the exact same title. It was *that* song plugger's job to learn all of the sheet music in the store and be able to play it for customers. The store's in-house song plugger spent his or her days at the piano, playing and singing whatever sheet music a customer wanted to hear. If the customer liked the song, a piece of sheet music would be sold. If enough customers bought sheet music of the same song in enough cities and towns across the country, that song was considered a hit.

The late 1800s was also the era when the theatrical genre known as vaudeville came into existence. Vaudevillians were troops of singers, musicians, dancers, comics, jugglers, acrobats, magicians, and other entertainers who traveled across the country putting on shows in local theatres and music halls.

So while some song pluggers were still traveling salesmen pitching sheet music to store owners, other song pluggers began pitching songs to vaudeville singers. And since New York City was home to vaudeville's booking agents, many vaudeville theatres, and the industry trade paper of that era—the *New York Clipper*—it also became home to most of the major music publishers, and therefore, home to most song pluggers.

Due to the fact that there was now an elaborate passenger train system across the entire country, vaudeville troops could perform in any town with a train station and a theatre. For music publishers, that meant every vaudeville theatre was filled with potential sheet-music customers. Therefore, the primary goal of the New York–based song plugger was to charm, woo, cajole, beg, or otherwise convince vaudeville singers to perform songs owned by the song plugger's employer, the music publisher.

As would later be the case with motion picture and television actors, as well as with performers on radio and recordings, the more popular vaudeville acts were the "stars" of their day. If a song plugger was able to convince one of those

Sheet music for the song "Pride of the Prairie (Mary)," with a photo of vaudeville star Cheridan Simpson on the cover.

stars to perform a song the plugger represented, the music publisher would often print sheet music of that song with the performer's picture on the cover. That way, when the vaudeville audience would see and hear that particular performer singing the song in person, those who wanted to be able to buy the sheet music of that song would go to the store, find the sheet with that performer's picture on it, and rack up another sale for the music publisher. Not only did the cover photo concept help to sell sheet music, it was also a way of enticing the performer to keep the song in the act (and maybe even be enough of an ego stroke to cause that performer to add more of the publisher's songs to his or her repertoire in exchange for more sheet-music cover photos).

It wouldn't be long though before twentieth-century technology would begin to impede on vaudeville's popularity. With both recordings and radio becoming exciting new forms of in-home entertainment in the 1920s, vaudeville began to lose a lot of its steam.

Just before the vaudeville genre died out in the 1930s (primarily because motion pictures were now being shown in the theatres where live performances had once been the main attraction), a Saginaw, Michigan, songwriter named Gerald Marks went to see Belle Baker performing at a vaudeville theatre in Detroit.

At the beginning of that decade, Marks and his partner, Seymour Simons, had written "All of Me"—a song they believed in so much that Gerald traveled from Michigan to New York to try to get it published. Over fifty years after that ill-fated trip, Gerald told me, "I was my own song plugger, pedaling that song up and down the street. Every single publisher I played it for turned it down. I only had enough money to stay in New York for a week, so once the money ran out, I went back to Saginaw.

> Not long after that, I saw that Belle Baker was going to be performing in Detroit. She was a huge star at the time—both in vaudeville and on Broadway. What happened next was a series of lucky accidents. The first accident was that I was able to get backstage. The second accident was that she had a piano in her dressing room.
>
> I started playing the song for her while she put her makeup on, and as I was singing, she suddenly burst into tears. Later I found out that the night I sang "All of Me" for Belle Baker, it was the first anniversary of her husband's death.
>
> She essentially became my song plugger, performing it on the radio that very night at the Fisher Theater in Detroit.

The song was so meaningful to Ms. Baker that she began to cry again as she sang "All of Me" in front of the live audience. Her tearful performance was picked up by the national press, making "All of Me" a very sought-after song by other artists. Within weeks, it was a No. 1 hit for Paul Whiteman and His Orchestra, with Mildred Bailey on vocals. Louis Armstrong's recording of the song came out less than a month after Whiteman's, and it, too, went to No. 1.

Over the years, "All of Me" would become one of the most recorded songs in the history of American popular music, being cut by over 2,000 artists including—you guessed it—both Frank Sinatra and Willie Nelson.

★ ★ ★ ★ ★

Music publishers and song pluggers had to adapt to the changing times, as did the stars of vaudeville. Visual artists such as jugglers, acrobats, and magicians were pretty much out of luck in the new world of radio and recordings, but many popular vaudeville singers developed even larger national followings thanks to these new entertainment formats.

A few years earlier, the US Copyright Act of 1909 had granted music publishers the right to be paid two cents for every "mechanical device" sold. Initially the law was specifically referring to a device called a piano roll. A piano roll looked like a scroll with a bunch of holes punched in it, and was used in player pianos. Player pianos were exactly that: self-playing pianos containing a pneumatic device that operated the piano keys via the holes in the piano rolls. Each perforation caused a specific note to be played.

Congress determined that publishers had created a monopoly in the marketplace by granting one specific piano roll company rights to their songs, to the exclusion of all other piano roll manufacturers. Therefore, the 1909 copyright law determined that two cents would be the statutory mechanical royalty rate all piano roll companies would be required to pay for each piano roll sold. As long as the piano roll manufacturer paid the two cents per sale, a publisher couldn't refuse to allow the piano

~ KNOW YOUR HISTORY ~

Today you can still apply song plugging ideas from the past to the present day. Gerald Marks managed to successfully pitch "All of Me" by getting an unplanned private meeting in the dressing room of one of the major stars of his day. I've been backstage with various recording artists on numerous occasions, and—although I didn't sit down at the piano and belt out a tune for them—I did find it to be the perfect time to let an artist know I had a song that was right for him or her. Most civilians (i.e., non–music industry people) think there's a giant party going on in the Green Room of every venue before and after a show. On more than one occasion, I've found myself to be the only person in the room with an artist while the opening act was onstage. Sometimes a backing musician or two might come in to pick through the food on the catering table, but more often than not, the Green Room party—if it happens at all—doesn't start until after the main act has left the stage. So right now you're thinking, "Hey man, how do you get in the Green Room in the first place?" You want shrewdness and chicanery? Get to know the soundman, or one of the roadies, or the lighting guy, or the bass player. Okay, maybe not the bass player. When you and the soundman stop by the Green Room for a carrot stick and a couple of purple M&Ms, introduce yourself to the star. It's always worked for me.

The people I admire most in the music business are the ones who know not just the current scene but who also have a good working knowledge of the past. You can't know where the music's going if you don't know where it's already been.

By now you've figured out that I'm a blatant and unapologetic name dropper. I didn't claw my way up the music industry mountain to hang out with a bunch of suits. If I wanted to spend my days with those kinds of folks, I would've gotten a job on Wall Street, had an ulcer by the age of twenty-five, and my first bypass before I turned forty. Who needs it? Not me and not you.

I had the privilege of dining with Michael Jackson on more than one occasion. At one of those luncheons, he started talking to me about Wynonie Harris and Roy Brown—two jump blues artists few people remember today. I was absolutely astounded. Michael Jackson knew the early history of the music that eventually evolved into the R&B of Michael's era. It pays to know your history.

roll company to manufacture rolls of that music publisher's copyrights.

Not long after the 1909 copyright law was enacted, cylinder recordings and 78-rpm discs overtook the popularity of piano rolls. Under the copyright law, recordings were also considered to be mechanical devices. Today, any device sold that contains a musical recording (including a digital download) requires the manufacturer or digital distributor to pay "mechanical royalties" for each copy sold and/or downloaded. Luckily, the rate—which changes every few years—is now substantially higher than two cents.

For song pluggers in the era of 78-rpm records and early radio, pitching tunes to what was left of the vaudeville circuit performers became much less important than trying to get the songs they represented cut by recording artists or performed on the radio (or better yet, both).

In 1914, the American Society of Composers, Authors and Publishers was formed. Known in the industry by its acronym, ASCAP, the organization was created to collect royalties for public performances of copyrighted works—another right granted by the 1909 copyright act.

An industry that had survived for decades on sheet music sales alone now had three separate income streams: print royalties (sheet music and songbooks), mechanical royalties, and performance royalties.

The good news for song pluggers was that they didn't have to be able to sing and play the piano anymore. The bad news was—with more money to be made in music publishing than ever before—the competition suddenly became much stiffer.

CHAPTER SEVEN

★ ✫ ★

By the time Jerry Leiber told me to pitch the Sinatra Song to Willie Nelson, the actual job title of "song plugger" had become pretty much passé in the music publishing business. Over time, a song plugger became known as a "professional manager." Later, song pluggers started having the word "creative" somewhere in their title—such as "Vice President of Creative Affairs." Some music publishing companies have lifted the initials "A&R" from record labels to refer to the people on staff who pitch songs. (*A&R* means "Artists and Repertoire." It originated as a record-company term that applied to those at the label who were in charge of determining what songs an artist was going to record. There are still plenty of executives at record labels that are called A&R men or A&R women, but it's been so many years since a record-company honcho picked all of the songs for an artist's album that some of today's A&R execs probably don't even know what the *A* and *R* stand for.)

Like I said earlier, in addition to those at music publishing companies who pitch songs to recording artists, there are also executives whose job is to attempt to get songs placed in motion pictures, television shows, commercials, video games, and other forms of media.

In my case, I might be the president of Leiber & Stoller Music Publishing, but when it came time to track down Willie Nelson and play "The Girls I Never Kissed" for him, my job was to be a song plugger.

★ ★ ★ ★ ★

Knowing I was in search of an artist who seemed to be on the road more than he was at home, I decided to check out pollstar.com, a website that lists the tour itineraries of literally thousands of performers. I sat at my computer and typed "Willie Nelson" into the search box, hoping against hope that he would be hitting Southern California very, very soon.

But it was not to be. According to the website, he had a gig in Ontario, Canada, that night. And as if that weren't bad enough, he was heading in the wrong direction—going from west to east across the entire breadth of Canada—while I was sitting in an office building less than ten miles from the Pacific Ocean.

In an effort to make myself feel better, I went to Willie's own website to see where he'd been before the Canadian tour had started. I was hoping for someplace like Europe or Japan. But no—of course not. His last show had been in Fayetteville, North Carolina, three weeks earlier. While I'd been busy forgetting that I was supposed to pitch the Sinatra Song to him, Willie had probably been hanging out in Texas or Maui with nothing to do for the last three weeks—lying in a hammock, smoking a joint, and wondering why nobody had pitched him any good songs lately.

I sat and stared at my computer screen, quietly mumbling "Holy crap!" I stood up and started walking back and forth across the room, adding the phrase "This is not good," as Willie's eyes seemed to follow me from the Wall of Fame while I paced.

Helen Mallory, who had occupied the office next door to mine for a decade and a half, strolled by. "What's not good?" she asked from the hallway.

I sat back down. "Was I really talking out loud?"

"Yep," she said as she walked into my office. "I believe the exact phrase was, 'Holy crap! This is not good.'—About a dozen times by my count."

She sat down across the desk from me while I told her the whole saga. She pondered my quandary for a minute. "Okay, I've given this some thought," she said, "and I've come to the only logical conclusion."

"Great! What is it?"

She stood up and walked to the door. When she turned her head, looking back at me over her shoulder, I could see great concern on her face as she whispered, "You're totally screwed." Then she gave me a little wave and a big smile before quickly ducking back into her office. Except for the big smile, it was like watching a loved one waving goodbye to a leper victim on the boat to Molokai.

"Holy crap!" I said. "This is *really* not good."

~ THE INTERNET ~ IS YOUR OYSTER

Nobody—especially not my son—wants to hear "When I was your age" stories. They're the worst. But even he couldn't control his laughter when I tried to explain to him what the world was like pre-Internet.

Today practically all of the information you need about an artist is literally at your fingertips. If you want to see and hear a particular performer, you're almost certain to find that act on youtube.com. Whether it's someone who has put out one self-released CD or someone who has scored dozens of hits over a long career, odds are they both have websites. So do all the major (and most minor) record labels, as well as music publishing companies, performing rights societies, and numerous other music business–related entities.

Before the Internet became a part of our lives, acquiring an artist's itinerary was not a two-minute task. Today, with very little effort, you can find out an artist's manager, booking agent, public-relations contact, record label, and virtually anything else you might need to know. Just a few years ago, you would've had to spend hours on the phone or searching through various industry publications to acquire the same information you can now locate in a matter of minutes. When it comes to song plugging, take advantage of all the modern-day tools at your disposal.

CHAPTER EIGHT

★ ✮ ★

The Sinatra Song is one of Leiber and Stoller's proudest achievements, and rightly so. They had already been writing songs together for thirty-six years when Frank Sinatra went into the studio to cut "The Girls I Never Kissed" for Reprise Records.

Jerry and Mike had become songwriting partners in 1950 when they were both just seventeen years old. Over the next couple of decades, they created some of the biggest hits in the history of rock & roll, pop, blues, R&B, and soul. Although they were hardly as famous as the acts that recorded their songs, the words and music the two of them wrote were known all over the world. It seemed that everybody loved the songs Leiber and Stoller provided for the biggest stars of rock & roll.

Well, not quite everybody. A lot of parents disapproved. And then there was Frank Sinatra. Frank *hated* rock & roll. In the late 1950s, he expressed his opinion on the subject in the pages of a magazine called *Western World*:

> My only deep sorrow is the unrelenting insistence of recording and motion picture companies upon purveying the most brutal, ugly, degenerate, vicious form of expression it has been my displeasure to hear—and naturally, I'm referring to the bulk of rock & roll. It fosters almost totally destructive reactions in young people. It smells phony and false. It is sung, played, and written—for the most part—by cretinous goons. And by means of its almost imbecilic reiteration, and sly, lewd—in plain fact—dirty lyrics, it manages to be the martial music of every side-burned delinquent on the face of the earth.

I'm not even sure what some of that means, but the gist of it is obvious: Frank Sinatra loathed rock & roll. And about Elvis Presley in particular, Sinatra once said, "His kind of music is deplorable—a rancid-smelling aphrodisiac." Elvis Presley was also one of the primary artists responsible for Leiber and Stoller's songwriting success in the 1950s and early 1960s.

But as the 1960s drew to a close, Jerry and Mike literally changed their tune. They stopped writing rock & roll and started focusing on more grown-up subject matter. In 1969—the year of the Rolling Stones' "Honky Tonk Women," and "Sugar Sugar" by the Archies—Leiber and Stoller scored a major hit with a partly sung/partly spoken work called "Is That All There Is?" Both musically and lyrically, nothing could have seemed more out of place on Top 40 radio. But a great song is always a great song, and Peggy Lee's recording of "Is That All There Is?" rode up the charts alongside Elvis, the Beatles, and Sly and the Family Stone, eventually garnering a Grammy for the woman who was old enough to be the mother of most of the other hit makers of 1969.

Leiber and Stoller wrote "The Girls I Never Kissed"—another one of their adult-oriented songs—with Frank in mind. But the hard part was finding a way to get the song to Sinatra. Luckily, Jerry and Mike were dining at the Friars Club in New York one day, sitting at a table next to one of the music business's legendary song pluggers, Frank Military. Tip of the iceberg: über–song plugger Military was responsible for Johnny Mathis recording "Misty," for Louis Armstrong recording "What a Wonderful World," for Barbra Streisand's record of "My Coloring Book," and for getting Sinatra to record "New York, New York."

When Jerry overheard Military complaining that the music business was driving him nuts, he turned to Frank's table and asked, "Why is that?"

"No one gives a shit about songs anymore," Military told him. "I can't even remember the last time I heard someone say, 'Frank, I have an absolutely gorgeous song that's actually intelligent and perfect for Sinatra.'"

Jerry's response, of course, was, "Frank, I have an absolutely gorgeous song that's actually intelligent and perfect for Sinatra."

After lunch, the three men strolled from the Friars Club back to Jerry's apartment. Leiber and Stoller played Military the song; a few days later, Military played it for Sinatra; and a few days after that, Sinatra was in the studio recording "The Girls I Never Kissed."

★ ★ ★ ★ ★

For the rest of his life—even though he had a repertoire of many, many hits from which to choose—Sinatra frequently sang "The Girls I Never Kissed" in his concert appearances. Always one to speak his mind, every time Sinatra introduced the song, he seemed to marvel at Leiber and Stoller's transformation from rock & roll writers to writers of the kind of songs that met with Ol' Blue Eyes' approval. In one memorable 1987 Carnegie Hall performance, he told the audience,

> We'd like to do a new song for you. It's a marvelous song written by a couple of kids who, strangely enough, used to write for Elvis Presley and do all those rock things—and suddenly they grew older and now they write pretty songs, ballads, you know, not the "Hound Dog" and "Wolf Dog" and all those other "mother's ass" things they used to do—*stupid*, goddamn songs. This, you might say, is reminiscent of a song like "September Song."

(Clearly, Sinatra's opinion of rock & roll hadn't softened over the years.)

Sinatra wasn't happy with the way his first recording of "The Girls I Never Kissed" had turned out, so he went back into the studio and cut the tune a second time. But soon after that second take, Sinatra parted ways with Reprise Records, the label he had originally formed in the early 1960s for himself and pals such as Dean Martin and Sammy Davis Jr.

"The Girls I Never Kissed" languished in the vaults until it was finally released in 1995 as part of a limited-edition twenty-CD retrospective of Sinatra's studio recordings for Reprise. The song was number 450 in a CD collection of 452 songs—third from the last on the twentieth CD. As a result, not many people had the opportunity to hear it.

There was no disputing that "The Girls I Never Kissed" was a great song—right up there with "Is That All There Is?" as far as Leiber and Stoller's more adult-themed songs were concerned. But just like the Peggy Lee standard, it couldn't be sung by a twenty-year-old. "The Girls I Never Kissed"—as Sinatra himself had pointed out at his Carnegie Hall concert—was like Kurt Weill and

Sheet music for Leiber & Stoller's "The Girls I Never Kissed," better known around the office as the "Sinatra Song."

Maxwell Anderson's "September Song." It would only work for an older man, and for someone who could sing convincingly about looking back at the missed opportunities in his life.

That meant one of the only singers besides Sinatra who could do the song justice was Tony Bennett. I had gotten the song to Bennett's manager on more than one occasion, going all the way back to the late 1980s, when it appeared that the Sinatra version might never be released at all. Tony's manager had told me from time to time that Bennett was seriously thinking about recording the song. But the years kept passing, Tony kept making albums, and "The Girls I Never Kissed" kept failing to make the cut.

And then came that fateful day at Jerry's dining room table, followed by the phone call from Mike about Jerry's displeasure over my having forgotten to hop on a plane and hand deliver the song to Willie Nelson—one of the few singers left on the planet who could do the song justice.

~USE YOUR EARS~

The world is filled with people who failed to reach their full potential simply because they didn't take advantage of a fleeting opportunity. Jerry Leiber could have overheard Frank Military's conversation at the next table and chosen to ignore it. If he had, there's practically no chance that Frank Sinatra would have ever recorded "The Girls I Never Kissed."

If you are going to be a song plugger, you have to constantly remain alert to any opportunity that might come your way. Wiretapping is bad form, but eavesdropping is entirely legal. If I find myself within earshot of a recording artist or a record producer—or anyone else who uses songs—I'm listening to what that person is saying, even though I'm smiling and nodding at the person who's actually talking to me. Emily Post—were she not dead—would no doubt frown upon my eavesdropping, but I do it because I know if opportunity rings the bell and I don't answer the door, it's not likely to stick around.

You have to use your ears to be able to hear a good song. Don't be afraid to use them to hear other people. If you say to a film director, "I couldn't help but overhear you saying that you're looking for a song to go over the closing credits of your next movie," he's not going to say, "Be gone, sycophant, and never let me see you cross my path again!" It's more likely that he'll respond in the affirmative and that an actual conversation will occur. And don't worry about him thinking you've been eavesdropping. He's much more likely to think he was just talking too loud.

CHAPTER NINE

★ ☆ ★

Back in 1978—the same year Willie Nelson's *Stardust* album was released—I was a disc jockey at a small radio station in Muscle Shoals, Alabama. Since my evenings were free, I decided to take a night course on music publishing at the University of North Alabama. Until I walked into class that first day, I had no idea what music publishing was. As soon as I learned there's an entire business that revolves around songs and songwriters, I knew that music publishing was the career path I wanted to stroll down.

Terry Woodford (class instructor, hit songwriter, music publisher, record producer, and studio owner) told us something on the first day of class that, technically, had nothing to do with the subject of music publishing per se. Practically, on the other hand, it had everything to do with music publishing. He made a statement that I had somehow gone through life without having heard up to that point. It was a simple, no-doubt ancient cliché, and the most important phrase I ever heard anyone say on the subject of the music business, or any business, for that matter: "It's not what you know—it's who you know."

Being the eager student that I was, I asked for clarification. Having spent so many years in school by that point, I was pretty convinced that nothing could be more important than "what you know." Luckily, Terry Woodford was a very patient man.

"Somewhere out there is an extremely gifted songwriter—maybe the greatest songwriter who ever lived," Terry said, "But we'll never have a chance hear what he's written, because he doesn't know anyone who can help bring his talent to the public's attention."

That's all it took. The light bulb over my head absolutely exploded. I could learn every last detail about the subject of music publishing—copyright law, royalty streams, licensing, song plugging, contracts, and all the rest—but it would be meaningless if I didn't develop the necessary contacts to get a job in music publishing. With the right contacts, I might be able to get my foot in the door of a music publishing company, but without developing relationships within that company, I probably wouldn't have an opportunity to advance to a higher position. Without even more contacts, I might not be able to find great songwriters

~IT'S NOT WHAT YOU KNOW—IT'S WHO YOU KNOW~

From this moment onward in your life, this phrase should be your mantra. Maybe you were lucky and heard it long before you were the age I was when Terry Woodford said it in my music publishing class. Maybe you were one of those really popular kids in high school practically born with this knowledge already ingrained in your cranium. Maybe you never heard it before you read this chapter. All I can tell you is this: no one who wants to be successful in any profession in life—with the sole exception of "professional hermit"—can live in a vacuum.

At the risk of sounding more than a tad egomaniacal, I think most people would agree that I turned out to be relatively successful in the music business. Prior to selling off a portion of our company in 2003 for tens of millions of dollars, I presided over one of the largest independent music publishing companies in America. For me though, it's never been about the prestige or the take-home pay (although you'll never hear any complaints from me on that issue). It's ultimately about the relationships I've developed over the years—the songwriters I've met, the other music publishers I've met, the people I brought into the industry who I've seen go on to great success, the friends I've made—actual, real-life stuff.

There's no doubt I could've "networked" my way to an even higher spot on the corporate food chain. In fact, I've turned down some pretty impressive jobs because I take great pleasure in being exactly where I am.

Most folks have to work for a living, and an awful lot of people are pretty miserable at their jobs. I've certainly met plenty of them, even in the music business. And I suspect their constant displeasure is brought about, at least in part, by their inability to understand the true meaning of the phrase, "It's not what you know—it's who you know."

to sign to that music publishing company. And without developing relationships throughout the whole music industry, I wouldn't meet the people I'd need to know to be able to pitch songs to them. All forward movement in the music business is about who you know.

I don't know if the word "networking" existed back in the 1970s. Today everybody knows what networking is, but to me that word seems to have a hollow, impersonal ring to it. Maybe it's just me, but I prefer the phrase "developing relationships" over "networking." When I hear someone say they're interested in networking, to me it sounds as if person A wants to use person B for the sole purpose of getting names, numbers, and email addresses from person B, so person A can then get in touch with person C, who might be able to hook him or her up with person D, who might be useful in some way to person A.

When those people hear the phrase "It's not what you know—it's who you know," it seems to me that they're hearing all the emphasis on the word *who*. In truth, it's not just *who* you know. It's who you *know*.

CHAPTER TEN

★ ★ ★

How do you get to know people in the music business? The short answer is "No cases are typical." If you live in New York, Nashville, Los Angeles, or one of the other cities with a major music scene, congratulations! You've already got an advantage over everyone else who doesn't live where you do.

If you're not living in one of the music business metropolises, you've got three choices: 1) Move to one, 2) be prepared to take extended trips to one, or 3) start your own music business scene where you currently live. (If you decide to go with number 3, I admire your entrepreneurial spirit. Be sure to write and let me know how it works out.)

When I decided to take the plunge, I dove into the deep end. I sold everything I owned, paid off all my debts, got on a bus, and moved to New York with $275 in a wallet I'd made out of duct tape. But I had one advantage that a lot of folks don't have. A friend of mine from college was living in a three-bedroom apartment in the borough of Queens. One of his two roommates had moved out, so I went to New York knowing I had a place to live.

In 1980, the rent for this particular three-bedroom apartment in Jackson Heights was a whopping $450 a month—less than the monthly fee it now costs to park a car in a Manhattan garage. My one-third of the rent for a bedroom that was just big enough to squeeze a bed into was $150 a month. That left me with $75 to my name. The first day I was there, my friend from college borrowed $20 from me. So by the end of my first day in the big city, I was down to 55 bucks. You want clichés? I was on top of the world! I was in the city that never sleeps, baby! Sinatra had told us all if we could make it there, we could make it anywhere. And I was there! Now all I had to do was that "make it" part and everything would turn out great.

Outside of my two roommates, I didn't know another soul in Queens, Manhattan, or any of the other boroughs. In fact, I didn't know anyone else in the entire state—or the surrounding states of New Jersey, Connecticut, and Pennsylvania. Clearly, I had my work cut out for me.

★ ★ ★ ★ ★

I knew from my music publishing course that *Billboard* was the primary music-industry trade magazine. In short order, I found out about the library at Lincoln Center, where you could go and read the latest issue of *Billboard* from cover to cover for free.

Not to keep showing my age, but in those days it cost sixty cents to take the subway from Queens to Manhattan. Every day I'd spend $1.20 to make the round trip. My $55 was being depleted rapidly, thanks in no small part to the fact that I discovered I also required at least one meal a day.

But I knew if I was going to meet people in the music business, I had to know who they were. *Billboard* had photos of those people. There were shots of record executives posing with artists who were holding gold records. There were pictures of music publishers standing over desks while their latest finds were signing publishing contracts. There were photos of managers backstage with the bands they were representing. And every photo had a caption—and all those captions listed the names and titles of all those people in the pictures. Now I'm not going to say that I tore out a lot of those captioned photos, put them in my pocket, and then quietly slipped out of the library—but if you ever go to the New York Public Library for the Performing Arts at Lincoln Center and dig through old *Billboard* magazines from 1980, there's a chance you might find a few pages missing.

I memorized the faces and titles of everybody in those *Billboard* photos. I memorized the acts they represented. I memorized the titles of the gold albums their acts were holding. I read about the record labels they worked for, or the

Lincoln Center—Home of the New York Public Library for the Performing Arts, where I spent my days memorizing the names and faces of every person in every photo in every week's issue of *Billboard*, the music trade magazine.

publishing companies they ran, or the hit singles they produced. In a matter of weeks, just as my money was running out, I knew who most of the major players were in the New York music industry. Now all I had to do was find a way to get them to know me.

When I moved to New York, I didn't just *want* to be in the music business. I was *determined* to be in the music business. I knew it wasn't going to be easy or instantaneous, but I also knew nobody was going to stop me. Years later, when I was writing a book about legendary guitarist Duane Allman, everyone I interviewed who had known him said virtually the same thing: Duane Allman was filled with drive and determination. Granted he had incredible talent, but he wouldn't have made it very far on talent alone. Duane wasn't just going to be the best guitar player in the world—he was going to make sure that everybody knew it. Even the people I interviewed who knew him when he was just a teenager said there was no doubt that he would make it. It wasn't about ego—it was about being strong-willed and going after what he wanted to achieve, never letting anything stand in his way.

In the handful of years that Duane Allman was on the scene, he formed the Allman Brothers Band, recorded such classic albums as *Live at the Fillmore East* and *Eat a Peach*, shared guitar duties with Eric Clapton on the album *Layla & Other Assorted Love Songs*, and became one of the most sought-after studio guitarists in the world. As if that weren't enough, he's credited with creating the musical genre known as Southern rock. And he did it all before dying at the age of twenty-four. Now that's a guy who was *driven*. When *Rolling Stone* came out with its list of the "100 Greatest Guitarists of All Time," Duane was ranked No. 2. Jimi

~ YOU CAN'T KNOW THE PLAYERS WITHOUT A SCORECARD ~

If you're in a crowded bar in Nashville and find yourself standing next to a country superstar, you're likely to recognize him. However, your chances of pitching a tune to said superstar under those conditions are pretty remote because 1) if they feel like talking to you at all, they're likely to tell you they can't accept unsolicited material, or 2) they might have one of their bodyguards remove you from the premises head first. On the other hand, it might turn out that they're in a great mood, find you to be a fascinating individual, and tell you to make an appointment with their manager, Bobby Joe Greenberg, who's somewhere in the very bar you're standing in—along with a few hundred other people.

At that point, the ceiling is not going to crack open, God's almighty hand is not going to descend from the sky, His long majestic index finger is not going to point to the superstar's manager, and a booming basso profundo voice is not going to shout from the heavens, "The man I'm pointing at is Bobby Joe Greenberg, the manager of the country superstar you met at the bar!"

You've got to know what old Bobby Joe looks like. If you do, you can find him, introduce yourself to him, tell him about the great conversation you just had with Mr. Country Superstar, and hand him your business card while keeping your hand out for his. Then you should whip out your cell phone and ask him for his office number and his cell number. He's in a bar, for Pete's sake! He's been drinking! Take advantage of his tipsiness. You can always feel guilty about it later. But whether he's stone drunk or cold sober, do everything in your power to make an appointment with Bobby Joe—preferably tomorrow morning so there'll still be a chance he'll remember who the hell you are.

If, on the other hand, you don't know what Bobby Joe looks like, I wish you the best of luck—because the chances of you finding him in a crowded Nashville bar are pretty damn slim.

Today the Internet makes putting names, faces, and titles together incredibly easy. Use any and every method available that will help you figure out who the players are.

Hendrix came in at No. 1. If Duane Allman had lived to see he'd come in second place, there's no doubt in my mind that he would've been royally pissed off.

The point is this: if you're wanting to be in the music business, you've got to want it with every ounce of your being. If you're already in the music business and that's not your attitude, good luck when the end of the year rolls around and those pink slips get handed out.

If you want to be a song plugger, you've got to have a lot more drive than all those music business executives sitting behind their desks. You've got to be on the streets, meeting and greeting, shaking babies and kissing hands—whatever it takes to get your songs heard.

CHAPTER ELEVEN

★ ✮ ★

So there I was in New York—no job, no prospects of a job, and very little job experience. I'd been a disc jockey at a couple of radio stations in Alabama, and I'd worked in a poultry plant one summer while I was in college. My prospects of finding a job as a radio announcer in Manhattan were identical to my chances of finding a poultry plant on Fifth Avenue.

But I had no desire to get back into the world of radio. I was young and single and simply wanted to spend my first few weeks soaking up the experience of living in such a magical place. Along with my frequent subway trips to the library at Lincoln Center, I walked all over the city, taking in everything from Central Park down to Washington Square Park—until I realized that the vacation fund was almost gone and it was time to find a job.

My roommate (who had, by this time, paid back the twenty bucks he owed me) told me he'd heard about a company that specialized in promotional activities. When I asked him to be a tad more specific, he said they hired people to pass out fliers on the streets of Manhattan. I opened my duct-tape wallet, stared at my last few dollars, swallowed my pride, and asked him for the address.

Getting hired wasn't a problem. The job requirements were pretty simple: 1) hold a stack of fliers in one hand, 2) take one flier with the other hand, 3) hold the flier out in front of you, 4) attempt to hand the flier to one of the people walking toward you. (The operative word here is "attempt." Manhattan pedestrians have a built-in talent for ignoring anyone trying to get their attention.)

My first week on the job, I was assigned to pass out fliers in front of the Empire State Building. My second week on the job, the promotion company sent me to pass out fliers at Rockefeller Plaza. My third week on the job, they sent me to pass out fliers in front of the fountain at Lincoln Center. I almost enjoyed that third week because it meant I could go to the library at lunchtime and study that week's *Billboard* photos.

At the end of the third week, I went to the promotion company's headquarters—a single room in a building near Times Square—to pick up my weekly paycheck. When I arrived, I was told I wouldn't be handing out fliers anymore.

"We've been watching you," my boss told me. "You're one of the few people we've ever hired who actually stayed and passed out the entire stack of fliers we gave you each morning."

"I am?" I asked, feeling more than a little creeped out by the thought of being spied on. "What does everybody else do?"

"Most of the other people we've hired pass out fliers for an hour or two and then toss whatever they have left in the trash. But you actually went wherever we told you to go, and then you did exactly what we'd asked you to do."

"Then why are you telling me you don't want me to pass out fliers anymore?" I asked, trying to keep my lower lip from trembling.

"Because our business is really growing. We're getting more and more clients who want to use our service, and we want to make sure the people we hire are doing their job. Starting next week, we're going to send you out with two other people. Your job will be to watch them like a hawk all day, making sure they pass out all of the fliers we give them every morning."

"So I just stand there all day and watch them?" I asked.

"Well you don't have to stand," my boss said. "There are benches at Rockefeller Plaza and Lincoln Center. We just want you to sit on a bench and keep an eye on your coworkers. Feel free to bring a book with you.

"Oh, and one more thing," he said. "We're giving you a raise."

I learned a lot of lessons passing out fliers on the streets of Manhattan—most of which also apply to song plugging. First of all, to do your job right, you've got to be where the people are that you're trying to reach. Secondly, most of those people are going to reject you because they don't want what you're trying to give them. Thirdly, it's a great feeling when somebody actually reaches out their hand and accepts what you're offering. Fourthly, you can't get depressed if they take a quick glance at what you've handed them and then throw it away. And fifthly, if you turn out to be really good at your job, you'll end up in management and get paid more money—to *not* do the very thing you were so good at in the first place.

The next time the music business collapses—and it will—feel free to come back and read the above paragraph again.

~NO JOB TOO SMALL~

The late Texas governor Ann Richards reportedly once said of George Bush, Sr., "He was born on third base and thought he hit a triple." Most of us spend years just trying to get to first base in our chosen profession. I'm sorry to have to say that getting on to any base in the music business is, in many ways, a lot harder today than it used to be.

But if you have the perfect combination of talent, drive, ambition, and luck, your chances are the same as anyone else in your position. If you don't live in a music center, the old cliché about the first step being the hardest is really true. I don't want to be responsible for a bunch of people reading this book, moving to a big city, and then ending up living in a cardboard box because things didn't work out, so I'll tread lightly here.

Please note, although I didn't show up in New York with a million bucks in my pocket, I did arrive with a place to live and enough money to survive for a few weeks. I also knew in my heart that I could always drag my ass back to Alabama and get another radio gig if things totally failed to work out. So if you're living in Humptulips, Washington, and you don't have a seriously large roll of bills in your pocket, it's not yet time for you to stick out your thumb and hitchhike to LA.

If, on the other hand, you're properly prepared to take the plunge and head for New York, Nashville, Los Angeles, or one of the other music hubs, be prepared to take any job you can to keep a roof over your head and food on the table.

If I hadn't taken the job passing out fliers on the streets of Manhattan, I never would have survived long enough to eventually get a job in the music business. To paraphrase B. B. King and plenty of other blues singers, I've paid my dues. If you weren't born on third base, you'll probably have to pay your dues, too. Just like it says on my handyman's business card, "No job too small."

CHAPTER TWELVE

As winter weather hit NYC in late 1980, the promotion company prepared to shut down for the season. When I asked my boss if he had any job suggestions, he asked, "Can you type?"* I told him that, indeed, typing was my best subject in high school. I wasn't kidding. "But can you type fast?" he asked.

"I was the fastest typist in my class—ninety-five words a minute," I said. My boss looked stunned.

"You mean to tell me you've been working outdoors in the flier racket when you can type ninety-five words a minute? There are temp agencies all over town that would kill for somebody who can type that fast."

....

* In case you're too young to remember—in the days before personal computers, people had to use typewriters. The typewriter keyboard was configured very much like computer keyboards are today, but the user typed words directly onto a piece of paper that was scrolled onto the typewriter roller. There was no such thing as spell check. If you didn't know how to spell something, you had to look it up in a dictionary. There wasn't a built-in thesaurus either, so you had to have one of those next to your dictionary. If you made a typo, the fancier electric typewriters would let you back up and type the same letter in white ink to make it disappear (sort of). Otherwise you used a product called Wite-Out, which was a white fluid you applied to the incorrectly typed letter with a tiny brush. And of course, cutting and pasting was not an option. If you decided your fourth paragraph should have been your third paragraph, you had to scroll the page out of the roller, wad it up in anger, throw it in the trashcan, and then start all over again. By the end of the 1980s, typewriters had been, for the most part, replaced by computers with word processing programs—and not a moment too soon.

"What's a temp agency?" I asked him.

"They're agencies that get people like you temporary jobs doing things like typing, filing, answering phones—you know, secretarial kind of work."

Somehow that didn't seem like a step up to me, but I really, really didn't want to go back to Alabama and admit defeat unless my prospects of survival became utterly hopeless.

When I got back to my apartment, I discovered that things were heading toward utterly hopeless faster than I'd imagined. On the very day I'd gotten the news that the "flier racket" was closing up for winter, one of my roommates announced that he would be moving out—immediately. In the blink of an eye, my already impossible-to-afford $150 a month share of the rent had become $225 a month. I'd been living hand to mouth during my short time in New York. Now I had no job and no idea how I was going to come up with the extra $75 every month. So I pulled out the Yellow Pages, looked under "Temp Agencies," and discovered there were literally dozens of them. The next morning, I got on the subway and headed into Manhattan with a list of temp agency addresses in my pocket.

The very first one I went to required me to take a typing test. When I turned in what I'd typed, the lady at the temp agency said, "You're done already?" Then she looked it over, smiled, and said, "So what kind of work would you like to do?"

I'd lived in New York for about four months, and this was the first time anyone had asked me that question. "I want to be in the music business," I told her.

She flipped through a bunch of index cards (remember, this was years before people had computers on their desks), pulled one out, and said, "Okay, here's a job you might like. It's a music publishing company down in the East Village. They need somebody for two days to type up mailing labels."

Two days! I suddenly understood why they were called "temp" agencies. She told me which subway to take, and which stop to get off. "Be there tomorrow morning at nine a.m.," she said.

★ ★ ★ ★ ★

The next morning, I was up early. I arrived at the music publishing company at eight forty-five. The name of the firm was Carl Fischer Music, which—I would

later learn— had been around since the late 1800s. The building I entered at
Cooper Square had been the home of the company since 1923. The place was so
old that the elevator had to be operated manually. It was like stepping into a time
machine and hitting the reverse button.

I told the elevator operator who I was and why I was there. He took me up
toward the eighth floor. First we went just above it. Then we went just below it.
Finally he was able to get the elevator floor even with the eighth floor, pulled the
doors open, and told me to see the receptionist.

When I stepped off the elevator, I was half expecting to see a bunch of men
and women dressed in business suits from the 1920s. I turned to my left, took
one look at the receptionist, and could not control my jaw as it began to drop
toward the floor.

The receptionist was dressed in modern-day attire—but she was sitting behind a switchboard! Until that moment I had only seen switchboards in the movies—really *old* movies. She was even wearing a headset. I stood there stupefied
as I watched her answer the phone. When it would ring, she would plug a cord
into the switchboard, ask who the person wanted to speak to, and then plug in
another cord to connect the two.

The receptionist turned and looked at me as if this was all perfectly normal.
"How can I help you?" she asked.

"I was sent over by a temp agency to type mailing labels," I told her.

She turned back to the switchboard, plugged in another cord, and told the
person on the other end of the line that the guy from the temp agency was in the
lobby. As she was talking into her headset, I suddenly had this horrible thought
that I was going to be led into a cubicle with a manual typewriter—perhaps an
old pre–World War II Underwood.

Just as the panic was beginning to set in, a kind-looking gentleman appeared
in the lobby. "You must be Randy," he said. "I'm David." Then he took me into an
office area that was filled with cubicles. Since I had arrived early, I was one of the
first people there. When he showed me the cubicle I'd be sitting in, I was extremely
relieved to see that the typewriter was of the relatively modern electric variety.

Next to the typewriter were an enormous stack of letters and several tall
stacks of blank mailing labels. "These are all letters from people who want to be

on our mailing list," David told me. "I need you to go through them, find the address on each one, and then type the address on one of these mailing labels. I told the temp agency that I needed someone for two days, but if it takes another day or so for you to do them all, that'll be fine." And then he quietly slipped back into his office.

I slid the first mailing label into the typewriter, set the tabs, looked at the address on the first letter, and began to type. By noon I was done. In front of me were four stacks of addressed mailing labels, each about a foot high.

I stood up, turned off the typewriter, and walked over to David's office. When I tapped on his door, I heard a faint "Come in." As I stepped into his office, David said, "Oh, I'm sorry. I completely forgot to tell you where the restroom is."

"That's okay," I said. "I actually came in to tell you I'm through."

There was a look of disappointment on his face. "You're quitting already?" he asked.

"No sir, I'm not quitting. I mean I'm done typing the labels."

He got up from his desk, walked to my cubicle, and looked at the four foot-high stacks of mailing labels next to my typewriter. He began thumbing through them, one stack at a time, as a broad smile spread across his face.

"Have a seat," he said, "I'll be right back."

I sat back down at my desk and watched David walk down the hall, knock on a door, and then disappear inside. A few minutes later he reappeared and motioned for me to come back to his office. By this time I'd realized the error of my ways. Instead of getting paid for at least two days' work, I'd probably managed to cut my pay down to a single half day. It turned out I couldn't have been more wrong.

"How would you like a job at Carl Fischer Music?" he asked me.

I was stunned. "Are you serious?" I asked him.

"Oh, I realize you're a young man and this place probably looks really old-fashioned to you, but I'd appreciate it if you'd consider coming to work here."

He was right that I was young, and he was wrong when he said the place "probably" looked really old-fashioned. I'd already seen the manually operated elevator and the ancient switchboard. This place was *definitely* old-fashioned.

But he had completely misinterpreted my question. Before I could clarify what I meant when I asked if he was serious, David made an offer.

"We can pay you $160 a week," he said.

Now I was more than just stunned—I was completely speechless. I sat there doing the math in my head. With $160 a week, even after taxes I'd be able to pay my monthly rent and still have around $300 left over for food and luxuries every month. Not only were my worries about having to move back to Alabama behind me, I was going to be able to live like a king! This was the greatest day of my life. As I sat there thinking about all the concerts, museums, and restaurants I'd be able to go to, David spoke again.

~ EVERY LADDER HAS A BOTTOM RUNG ~

Bill Clinton, George Stephanopoulos, and Kris Kristofferson were all Rhodes scholars. Which one ended up becoming a janitor at a Nashville recording studio? The one who wanted to be in the music business. Kris believed—and rightly so—that the lowest job in the music business is still a job in the music business.

If you want to be a song plugger—whether that means trying to get your own songs to the artists who matter, or trying to become a song plugger for a music publishing company—it's highly unlikely that you're going to get many people to pay attention to you if you have no track record in your chosen profession.

So how do you get a job in the music business when you've had no previous music-related job experience?" In my case, I used my only (and now totally obsolete) skill set: my ability to type ridiculously fast. A few years later, after I'd moved on up the music-biz ladder, a young man came to my office one day offering to write press releases about my company for free. Did I throw him out on his ear? Of course not. He took his talent for writing press releases and eventually became a major player for one of the music-based television networks.

If you have a talent or a skill that will get you in the door, use it. Kris Kristofferson wasn't the only person who began his career at a recording studio. One of the most successful song pluggers I know of in Nashville knew enough about technology to get a gig engineering demo sessions. Who do you meet at demo sessions in Nashville? The obvious answer is singers, musicians, and songwriters. Hmmm, wonder if any of those folks could turn out to be useful? Many a demo singer has ended up getting signed to a major label. I think you get my point.

Kris Kristofferson would go on to become one of the most successful country songwriters of his generation—but when he first arrived in Nashville, he was wise enough to know that the first step up the music business ladder is the bottom rung.

Always remember this: even if you have to start at the bottom, you're one rung higher than you were.

"Okay, look, I can offer you $180 a week, but you can't tell anybody else here what your starting salary is, because if you do, all the other people I've hired in the last year will be demanding raises."

Incredibly, he had taken my lengthy silence to mean that I thought his first offer was too *low*. Who was I to let him think differently? I stood up, shook his hand, and said, "You've got a deal."

"I'm glad to hear it." And then he said the one sentence I'd been waiting to hear for a long time: "Welcome to the music business."

CHAPTER THIRTEEN

★ ★ ★

I used to stammer a lot. Imagine Colin Firth in *The King's Speech* but with a thick Southern accent. As it turns out, I didn't need Geoffrey Rush to tutor me. All I needed was a microphone. Back in my disc jockey days, my immediate family was stunned to discover that I could actually talk on the radio without sounding like a combination of Porky Pig, Donald Duck, and Foghorn Leghorn. Soon after my music publishing book came out in 1990, requests for me to speak at music conferences, workshops, and seminars came fast and furious. Luckily, at these events a microphone was always provided for me to speak into. Over the course of the last couple of decades, I've spoken at events in New York, Nashville, Memphis, Los Angeles, Atlanta, and other cities around the country, as well as the UK. I even once spoke at Harvard Law School—an event so monumental that I actually cut off my outdated ponytail before getting on the flight to Boston.

Most music workshops and seminars have the obligatory "Q&A" period. Every one of us who ends up on a dais looking out at all those (mostly) young faces eager for knowledge knows there are two guaranteed questions that we'll be asked. One (from the singers and songwriters in the crowd) is "Can I send you some of my songs?" The other (from the would-be music executives in attendance) is "How do I get where you are?" The answer to the first question pretty much depends on the mood of the speaker at that precise moment. The answer to the second question is a little more complicated.

As I said earlier, I spent quality time memorizing the faces of all those mu-

~ PAR TOUS LES ~ MOYENS NÉCESSAIRES

There isn't any one specific way to get into the music business, there isn't any one specific way to pitch songs, and there isn't any one specific way to meet the people you want to pitch songs to. Remember the line scrolling along the bottom of my TV set? "No cases are typical." You have to find your own way to get both feet in the door—and then you have to work your butt off to keep from getting both feet (as well as the rest of you) escorted back out that door.

In his 1948 play *Les Mains Sales*, Jean-Paul Sartre—the noted French existentialist philosopher, playwright, novelist, critic, and so forth—managed to answer the ultimate question about plugging songs when he coined the phrase "Par tous les moyens néces-saires." A few years later, human rights activist Malcolm X would translate it into English: "By any means necessary."

My experiences are pretty much mine alone. Being a song plugger often requires craftiness—the same kind of craftiness I used in my early New York days to get myself into any room where I knew I'd be able to find and meet important executives in the music business. To paraphrase Gordon Gekko, "Craftiness is good." With a little inge-nuity, you can devise your own ways to get to know the people who can help you. Recording artists, record execu-tives, artist managers, and the other people you need to meet aren't going to come looking for you. You have to find them—by any means necessary.

sic industry bigwigs whose pictures appeared in *Billboard*. The next trick was trying to figure out how to meet them in person. So where would they be? In New York, they'd be in their offices during the day. I was out of luck there because I was busy passing out fliers (or oversee-ing my coworkers passing out fli-ers) my first few months in the Big Apple. Once I got the job at Carl Fischer, I was in the music busi-ness (albeit some strange throwback to another era), but I was working all day—on the Lower East Side to boot—so there was no way I could make appointments to see anyone in Midtown Manhattan during my lunch hour. Not that anyone would've taken me up on a lunch invitation in the first place.

Since meeting music indus-try people during the daytime was out of the question, I decided that meant only one thing: I'd have to meet them at night. (Ah, the beauty of youthful determination.) In New York, Los Angeles, and Nashville, there are numerous music indus-try–related black tie events going on throughout the year. Back in the early 1980s, security at these func-tions wasn't particularly tight. Any

Malcolm X—"By any means necessary."

guy in a tuxedo could walk in uninvited and mingle with the invited ones. And any guy working on the Lower East Side could go to one of the nearby vintage clothing stores and buy an ancient tuxedo jacket for around five bucks. Finding tuxedo pants was another matter. I've never understood why the jackets were available by the truckload but tuxedo pants were as scarce as hen's dentures. Luckily, black electrical tape wasn't so hard to find.

It wasn't difficult at all to scope out when and where ASCAP, BMI, and other music industry events would be taking place. Usually a lot of those functions would appear in the calendar section of *Billboard*. Once I knew "when and where," I'd don my one white shirt and my one clip-on bowtie, pull on my one pair of black pants (after having carefully affixed the black electrical tape down the sides of each leg), throw my vintage $5 tuxedo jacket over my shoulder, and head to the party.

No one ever checked my name at the door. No one ever turned to me and said, "Pardon me, but is that black electrical tape running down the sides of your pants?" No one ever grabbed me by the nape of my $5 tuxedo jacket and threw me out into the street. I was never brave enough to actually sit down at a table once the dinner got underway. This was a cocktail-hour-only move. And speaking of cocktails, I was happy to discover that the drinks at these events were frequently free!

My plan was simple: get in the door, go to the reception area, introduce myself to as many people I recognized from their *Billboard* photos as possible, and when the lights started blinking to indicate it was time for everyone to move into the ballroom—get out.

This is not a method for meeting people in the music business that I'd recommend today. Security is much tighter, and the consequences of getting caught could end up being severe. On the other hand, you could end up getting your own reality TV show, so who knows?

CHAPTER FOURTEEN

★ ✪ ★

There's an old adage among radio personalities that goes like this: "If you haven't been fired, you haven't been in radio long enough." There are plenty of variations on the same theme: "If you haven't been fired five times, you really haven't been in radio." Another one is "If you haven't been fired, you're nobody." My personal favorite was always: "If you haven't been fired, you will be."

Clearly I was never meant to make it as a radio personality, because I managed to move from one DJ job to the next of my own accord. I can't think of too many other fields of employment where keeping your job qualifies you as a failure. As far as my days at Carl Fischer are concerned, I'm not sure if my brief run there would qualify as a failure or a success—or, considering the relative insignificance of the job, whether it really matters or not—but I sure managed to go out in a blaze of glory. My old radio friends would've been proud.

I was employed in the lowest ranks of the music publishing business, but I was determined to work hard, keep getting to know more and more people in the industry, and ultimately become one of those people who had their photograph in the pages of *Billboard*.

I knew I had some sort of talent, but at Carl Fischer, the only talents being put to use were my abilities to answer the phone, type, and put things in filing cabinets. I didn't even have a business card with my title on it. In fact, when I asked my first boss there what my title was, he said, "You don't have a title. You're an administrative assistant."

"Well, isn't that a title?" I asked.

"No, it's not," he said. "It's a job description."

So I decided to take the words of Martin Luther King Jr. as my inspiration: "If a man is called to be a street sweeper, he should sweep streets even as Michelangelo painted, or Beethoven composed music, or Shakespeare wrote poetry. He should sweep streets so well that all the hosts of heaven and earth will pause to say, 'Here lived a great street sweeper who did his job well.'"

If administrative assistant was what I was called to be, then I was going to be the best one in Manhattan—or at least the best one on the Lower East Side. I developed such a reputation for my typing skills at Carl Fischer that the executives started fighting over me. Within less than a year, I was administrative assistant to the general manager of the whole damn company. Only the company's president and vice president ranked above him.

By this time, I had worked for so many different executives that I had gotten a pretty good grasp of the various divisions of a music publishing company, as well as how each of those divisions is run. I was young and full of confidence, and I truly believed I could easily step into the shoes of some of the executives I'd worked for. But every time one of those executives moved on to another job, a new executive got hired from the outside, usually from one of Carl Fischer's competitors. And I, in my youth and fury, began to get pissed.

Then, in late June of 1981, I read a commentary in *Billboard* written by Charles Koppelman. At that time, Koppelman was a major player in the music publishing business. The premise of his commentary was that there were very few "music-minded men" left in the music business. (Clearly chauvinism was still alive and well in the early 1980s.)

In my aforementioned youth and fury, I took umbrage with a portion of Koppelman's complaint. As soon as I finished reading the article, I scrolled a piece of paper into my typewriter and let my feelings fly—at ninety-five words a minute.

"Charles Koppelman spoke the truth, for the most part, in his commentary on the lack of music-minded men in the music industry," I wrote.

> From an insider's view, I must agree whole-heartedly that creative music men in *management positions* are, indeed, an "endangered species."

However, Mr. Koppelman and I "sing a different tune" as it were on the question of the actual existence of creative personnel. We are here and we exist in great numbers under the awesome weight of uncreative management . . .

So, to get our foot in the door, we settle for low-salary jobs with titles such as administrative assistant, and thank God we had the foresight to take a typing course somewhere along the way.

Thus, our only way to move to an eventual management position of our own is by playing "Superball" with our careers. The idea is to jump from company to company as the years pass, hoping to vault a little higher with each bounce until we reach a level equal to our skills and creative abilities.

I wrote paragraph after angry paragraph, concluding with: "If, as Mr. Koppelman states, 'It is becoming apparent that the music industry is in a crisis situation,' then it's time to try new tactics. Give those of us who are talented and creative—those of us who are music-minded—the chance we deserve."

When I finished that last paragraph, I scrolled back up to the top of the page and entitled the piece "A Corollary to Koppelman," by Randall Poe.

The editorial page in the magazine said that all submissions should be sent to Is Horowitz, Commentary Editor. I pulled out an envelope, typed Is's name and address on it, and put "A Corollary to Koppelman" in the mail that afternoon.

The next day my phone rang. The friendly gentleman on the other end of the line was Is Horowitz himself. "Mr. Poe, I love what you wrote," he told me, "And I want to run it in an upcoming issue of the magazine."

A year earlier I was memorizing photos in *Billboard* at the Lincoln Center library—now I was going to be in it! "Thanks, Mr. Horowitz. That's great news," I said.

"There's just one thing I wanted to mention before the issue goes to press. I'm presuming you'll want us to attribute the piece to 'An anonymous administrative assistant in the music publishing business' or something similar."

I was stunned. "Why would I want you to do that? Don't you think my article makes a valid point? Don't you think it's the absolute truth?"

Is Horowitz took a fatherly approach as he said softly, "Yes, I do. But if we put your name on the article, son, you're likely to get fired."

"You might be right," I said, "But I'm willing to take that chance. It would kill me to have something I wrote appear in the pages of *Billboard* magazine and not have anyone know I wrote it."

"I admire your confidence," he said. "Look for it in the issue coming out on July 4th."

July 4, 1981, was a Saturday. When I arrived at my desk the following Monday, I waited impatiently for the mail to show up. *Billboard* always came with the rest of the general manager's mail, but on this day of all days, it wasn't there. I would find out—in very short order—that the vice president of the company had intercepted the magazine on its way to my desk because, unbeknownst to me, Carl Fischer's marketing department had chosen to place an ad in that very week's issue. The ad that the vice president wanted to see was on page 6. The commentary he wasn't expecting to see was on page 16.

As the morning wore on, various executives began strolling into the general manager's office, each one giving me a stern look as he or she passed my cubicle. Finally they all emerged, giving me *really* stern looks as they passed by me a second time.

A few minutes later my phone rang. It was the assistant to the vice president of the company, telling me that the vice president wanted to see me in his office immediately. During my year at Carl Fischer, I had dreamed of the day the vice president would call me into his office to tell me I was getting a promotion. The missing *Billboard* and the stern looks I'd gotten were a pretty clear indication that I was being summoned to receive less pleasant news.

When I walked into the vice president's office for the first and only time, he didn't even ask me to sit down. "I read what you wrote in *Billboard*," he said. "I would fire you right this second, but the president is out of the country for the next two weeks, and I want to give him the privilege of reading your commentary and firing you himself upon his return. My advice to you is to start looking for a new job immediately."

At the time, I was truly shocked by the events of that day. All these years later, I honestly can't imagine what I thought was going to happen when that issue of *Billboard* hit the newsstands. It's not like Is Horowitz didn't warn me.

Ironically, being forced to seek new employment would lead me to a job in a completely different area of the entertainment industry—and would ultimately lead to my going to work for Leiber and Stoller.

~BELIEVE IN YOURSELF~

In 1964, Supreme Court Justice Potter Stewart defined "hardcore pornography" with the famous line "I know it when I see it."

I don't know how to define overconfidence, but we all know at least one person in our lives who has a huge dose of it. There's a thin line between believing in yourself and being overconfident, but it's not easy to know where one ends and the other begins.

When I wrote that commentary in *Billboard*, I honestly believed every word of it was truthful and accurate. Decades later, I haven't changed my mind. Would I do it all again if I'd known it would mean having to look for another job? I doubt it. Luckily, back in 1981 I still had a massive amount of naïveté on my side.

If you're a songwriter, you have to believe in your songs. If you're a song plugger, you have to believe in your ability to match a potential hit song with the exact artist who can make it a hit, and then find a way to get that song to that artist.

I've never met a successful songwriter or a successful song plugger who didn't believe in his or her own talents. Unfortunately, that doesn't mean they wrote nothing but hits or that every song they pitched got cut. In fact, it's safe to say that the batting average of both camps is pretty low. But the songwriters and song pluggers who did find success on some level were all confident in their abilities.

When I experienced the negative response my commentary got, I had to face the unpleasant fact that the people I was working for definitely didn't have confidence in my abilities. Instead of taking their opinions to heart, I remained totally confident that I was right.

It's never easy when others don't believe in you. But if you are determined to be a success, you only have to be concerned with what one person thinks. Believe in yourself.

The New York Times (by Lee Romero)

ATED SCHOOL: Virginia Holton, 13, with her father, Linwood Holton Jr., in Richmond. Blacks greatly outnumber whites. Dispatch is on Page 20.

cas Guilty of Plotting
ther Murder Case

By JOSEPH LELYVELD
Special to The New York Times

N, Aug. 31—A Sentencing on his conviction

RATIONING URGED
FOR OIL AND COAL

Public Power Group Warns

Ne
L

Signa
U.S

JERU
rael to
Truce S
today
had de
ther d
and
launchi
length
bank o

The
since t
tary st
United
came
Govern
portedl
tions w

Prem
trade u
ing th
"difficu
United
garded
ministr
to sa
agreem
change
of a 2
each si
United

LATE CITY EDITION

Weather: Sunny, unseasonably cool today; clear tonight. Fair tomorrow. Temp. range: today 74-59; Monday 2. Temp.-Hum. Index yesterday. Full U.S. report on Page 70.

15 CENTS

CHAPTER FIFTEEN

I took the advice of Carl Fischer's vice president to heart. My last paycheck was only two weeks away, so I knew I'd have to move fast. The *New York Times* always had a huge "Help Wanted" section in the Sunday classified ads. All of the job openings were given headings, so I bought the paper, opened it to the classifieds, and looked for the heading "Music." That week there was a single listing. It read, "Assistant to Executive Director, National Academy of Popular Music/Songwriters Hall of Fame."

The following morning, I went back to my cubicle at Carl Fischer. It was a week late, but someone had been kind enough to put the previous week's well-worn issue of *Billboard* on my desk, with an unsigned note attached that said, "Good luck. We'll miss you."

I immediately called and made an appointment with the executive director of the Songwriters Hall of Fame. Since I was on my way out the door anyway, I didn't mind skipping out for a couple of hours to seek new employment.

My audition for the job consisted of taking rapid dictation and typing a fictional letter to Marvin Hamlisch. To this day, I've always believed I ended up with the gig not only because I could type so fast but also because I was probably the only person applying for the job who could spell Hamlisch.

★ ★ ★ ★ ★

Shortly after I went to work as the executive director's assistant, the organization's board of directors held its monthly meeting at the Songwriters Hall of Fame Museum at One Times Square—the building probably best known as the place the big ball drops every New Year's Eve. The executive director brought me into the boardroom and introduced me to everyone. Every single person in the room was at least twice my age. More than one was three times my age. And believe it or not, one was very close to being four times my age.

After the meeting was over, one of the board members—songwriter/folk singer Oscar Brand—came into my little office, sat down, and said, "I'm going to give you a piece of advice. To be successful in the music business, you have to develop relationships. As of right now, your job is to get to know every member of the board. Don't just say hello to them once a month. Get to *know* them."

Get to *know* them. As soon as he said those words, my mind went back to Terry Woodford's statement of enlightenment in my music publishing class: "It's not what you know—it's who you know." When Oscar left my office that day, I resolved to follow his advice. Although it took a few weeks, I truly got to know every one of those men and women who sat on the board of directors.

The board members weren't people I was interested in networking with in an effort to bounce to another job somewhere. These were people I wanted to

Oscar Brand (L) lets Roger Deitz touch his Peabody.

know. Some were music publishers, and some were in other aspects of the entertainment business, but most of them were songwriters who had written many of the greatest standards in the history of American popular music. I was honored to have the opportunity not only to meet them but also to eventually be able to call most of them my friends—even if one of them was old enough to be my great-grandfather.

One day I was having lunch at the Century Club with Robert Sour, the man who cowrote the standard "Body and Soul." The next evening, I was having dinner at the resplendent apartment of "All of Me" cowriter Gerald Marks. Other days I would dine at the Carnegie Deli with the organization's president, legendary lyricist Sammy Cahn. I became close friends with Leonard Feist, who at that time was the president of the National Music Publishers Association (and whose father, Leo Feist, had owned one of the largest music publishing companies in the world in the 1920s). In fact, Leonard was one of the people I'd first met at a function back when I'd been crashing cocktail hours in my fake tuxedo. One of my favorite board members was Irv Lichtman, who would later become deputy editor of *Billboard* magazine. (Long after I had left the Hall of Fame and gone to work for Leiber and Stoller, Irv would write a feature article about me in *Billboard*. Turns out both Oscar Brand and Terry Woodford were right. Getting to know people and develop relationships with them did, indeed, result in good things.)

Following Oscar and Terry's advice also paid off in a way I never would've imagined. Having been no more than a sort of glorified secretary to the executive director for three months, I thought my job might be over when my boss unexpectedly decided to leave the organization. After all, whoever the new executive director was going to be, that person might very well bring in his or her own personal assistant.

When the board of directors convened to determine what to do about the unanticipated vacancy, I wasn't invited into the meeting as I had been in the past. While they met, I sat at my IBM Selectric II, typing out my résumé for the second time in three months. But when the meeting ended, Sammy Cahn—who as president of the organization also chaired the board meetings—stuck his head in my office, pointed a finger at me, and said, "Okay, Poe, you're it." Then he headed for the elevator. I honestly didn't know what he meant until Oscar Brand walked into my office with a big smile on his face. "Looks like you actually followed my advice," he said. "When your name was submitted to the board to be considered for the post of executive director, there was not one dissention. The vote was immediate and unanimous. Congratulations."

It's not what you know—it's who you know. In this particular case, those words were literally true, because I knew absolutely nothing about being the executive director of anything—certainly not executive director of one of the most important songwriter organizations in the country. I'd only had three months to figure out what I was supposed to be doing as the executive director's *assistant*. But the job was mine, and I was happy to take it.

~ YOU LIKE ME! YOU REALLY LIKE ME! ~

Real songwriters have this uncontrollable urge to write songs, along with an equally uncontrollable desire for other people hear what they've written. All good song pluggers want to take songs and try to find homes for them. Frequently a songwriter is his or her own best song plugger. Whether you're a songwriter, a song plugger, or both, you have to be—there's just no other way to say it—likeable.

When I had the opportunity to hang out with the various board members of the Songwriters Hall of Fame, I enjoyed every minute of it. As usual, I was lucky. I didn't have to pretend to be enjoying myself. I really was having a great time. They all had amazing stories to tell me, and I hung on every word. I wasn't faking it. I found these men and women to be really likeable people. And apparently, they found me to be the same.

If I'd spent the whole time yawning while they were talking, I doubt if they would have thought I was the right guy to be named the organization's executive director. In fact, I'm pretty sure I would've remained—at best—the assistant to whomever was hired to be the new executive director. In short, I didn't get the gig because they thought I knew how to fill the position. I was given the position for no other reason than the fact that they liked me.

Later in my career, I discovered that not everyone is as entertaining as an eighty-five- year old songwriter with a lifetime of stories to share. On many an occasion, I have found myself stuck in a lengthy afternoon meeting with some incredibly boring jerk. But I've never yawned. As far as that pompous jackass across the table from me was concerned, I thought he was the most interesting person I'd ever met in my life.

If you're pitching a song to someone in person, the person you're pitching to has to be the most wonderful human being you have ever had the pleasure to have met. When it matters, ingratiate yourself. You can always yawn later.

CHAPTER SIXTEEN

★ ★ ★

Not long after my unexpected promotion, it was time for the annual election of new Songwriters Hall of Fame inductees. Although I'll be the first to admit I honestly don't remember coming up with the idea, not too many years ago, one of the old (and I do mean old) Songwriters Hall of Fame board members told me that Bob Dylan was put on the 1982 ballot at my suggestion. (Not that it would've taken Stephen Hawking to figure out that Dylan deserved to be on the ballot his first year of eligibility.) Bob was easily elected that year, along with Paul Simon, Jerry Herman (*Hello, Dolly!*, *Mame*, *La Cage aux Folles*), and others. Harold Arlen—who wrote dozens of standards including "Somewhere Over the Rainbow," "Stormy Weather," and "That Old Black Magic"—received the Johnny Mercer Award (the organization's highest songwriting honor), and Dinah Shore received the Academy's Lifetime Achievement Award.

Dylan's people informed me that they probably wouldn't know whether or not Bob would be coming to the induction dinner until the last minute. The awards dinner was scheduled to take place that year on Monday, March 15th, at the New York Hilton. On Friday the 12th, I got a call from one of Dylan's staff saying that Bob's suit had just arrived at his office—a pretty good indication that Bob would be following it shortly. The main thing, I was told, was that it was imperative I work out an arrangement with the hotel to be able to slip Bob Dylan into the reception area in a manner that would keep the press from jumping all over him the second he arrived at the hotel.

I rushed over to the Hilton and met with hotel personnel who showed me the back entrance. Then they took me through a labyrinth of underground hallways that—after numerous twists and turns—eventually led to an elevator that opened up right next to the reception area. That weekend I tossed and turned in my sleep, each night dreaming of being trapped in an endless maze with Bob Dylan, who kept saying to me, over and over, "Something's happening here, but you don't know what it is, do you, Mr. Poe?"

★ ★ ★ ★ ★

On the evening of the awards dinner, my fiancée, Mina Yasuda, and I arrived at the New York Hilton. (By this time I had enough money to actually rent a tuxedo. The days of black electrical tape down the sides of my pants legs were behind me.) The Hall of Fame's PR director, Bill Feingold, was in charge of telling me when Bob Dylan had arrived at the back entrance. I was a nervous wreck, desperately trying to remember all the twists and turns of those seemingly endless hallways I was supposed to lead Bob through.

I was thrilled when I saw Woody Guthrie's widow, Marjorie, arriving at the event. Woody Guthrie had been one of Dylan's earliest musical influences, so it was fitting that Mrs. Guthrie would be among that night's attendees. I was walking over to introduce myself to her when Bill Feingold came barreling toward me at a near-gallop, practically shouting, "He's here!"

I took a deep breath and began walking toward the elevator at a pretty rapid clip when Bill stepped in front of me. "No, I mean he's here! He's already at the reception!"

I grabbed Mina's hand and pulled her into the room where the cocktail hour was in full swing. To our left were dozens of men in tuxedos and women in fancy dresses. To our right were more of the same. Directly in front of me—standing all alone—was *the* Bob Dylan, wearing a gray pinstripe suit and a black shirt unbuttoned halfway down his chest. I had no idea how he'd gotten there. It was as if he'd simply materialized from Scotty's transporter room right into the middle of the cocktail party. I looked at the barrage of photographers cloistered at the other end of the long room and realized they hadn't spotted him yet, so I moved fast.

My mission was to get Bob backstage for a few quick photos with Sammy Cahn—photos to be taken by Sam Teicher, the Hall of Fame's official photographer. After that, my job was to escort him to his table in the ballroom while everyone else was filing into the ballroom from the reception area.

I introduced myself to Bob, introduced Bob to Mina, and then sent her off to find Sammy Cahn and Sam the photographer. As Bob and I stood there staring at each other, I said, "Is there anything I can get for you?"

"Yeah," he said in that perfect, nasally Bob Dylan voice. "I'd like to get a picture of me with Dinah Shore."

For a second I thought he was surely pulling my leg, but he'd said it with such a straight face that I decided he just might be serious. At that moment, my fiancée arrived with Sammy Cahn and his wife, Tita. I did the introductions and then told Sammy, "Bob would like to get his picture taken with Dinah Shore." Without missing a beat, Sammy waved Bill Feingold over. "Go get Dinah and tell her I need her in the kitchen right now."

Sammy motioned for the four of us to follow him. Then he turned to me and sang so softly that only I could hear him: "Dylan's in the kitchen with Dinah . . ."

The kitchen entrance was discretely hidden from the ballroom by a curtained partition. Decades later, I can still recall the look of shock on Dinah Shore's face as she came around the corner of the partition and saw Bob Dylan standing there.

By the time Dinah arrived, Sam Teicher had already taken a few shots of Bob with Sammy Cahn. Just as Sammy stepped out of the way so Bob could get his picture taken with Dinah, I heard a noise that sounded like 10,000 termites boring through rotten wood. I turned around and saw dozens of photographers and guys with video cameras fighting their way through the nearest door and then pouring into the small space between the ballroom and the kitchen. Word had gotten out that Bob was in the building, and the photographers appeared none too happy about having been kept out of the loop. Bob and Dinah took it all in stride. They'd both been dealing with the paparazzi for years. I, of course, had never seen anything like it before in my life, and made the near-fatal mistake of trying to get the photographers and video cameramen to back off. I was unsuccessful, to put it mildly.

Just as the gang with cameras began closing in around us, an announcement came over the PA system saying that it was time for everyone to find their tables in the ballroom because dinner was being served. Naturally, Bob and Dinah

Bob Dylan gets his wish.

started heading toward their assigned seats. To my dismay, the photographers and videographers all followed Bob, who, of course, was sitting at table number 1 in the very front of the room. As I tried to stop the rushing hoard, I felt like Kevin Kline's character in *A Fish Called Wanda*—feet stuck in cement with a bulldozer coming straight toward me.

My personal opinion about the paparazzi "profession" was formed that night. Most of these people weren't photographers. They were animals in search of prey, with no regard for anything or anyone. A couple of them were real pros—well-known photographers I actually recognized who weren't pushing and shoving—but the rest could best be described as vicious. I watched as they used their elbows to knock elderly men and women out of their way in an effort to get closer to their target. As I stood facing them, reminding them—rather loudly—that only invited guests were allowed into the ballroom, they shoved me backwards and yelled at me to get out of the way. When a couple of them started kicking me in the shins, I began to get a tad pissed. Bob might not have needed a bodyguard that night, but I certainly could've used one.

When Dylan finally reached his table and sat down, things only got worse. The photographers literally surrounded his table. The constantly flashing cameras made that tiny section of the ballroom light up like the nightly fireworks display at Disneyland. One of the ladies sitting at the table next to Dylan's glared at me and said, "How could you let something like this happen?"

As I held my hand over the two camera lenses closest to me, I gave her a quick glance and said, "Feel free to join me because I can't stop these bastards by myself." At that point, the cavalry arrived in the form of hotel waiters—men and women whose job it is to move anybody who might be preventing them from getting the food to the table.

The waiters were better than security guards, causing the photographers to finally slither out of the room. As I took a deep breath and started to head toward my own table, I momentarily froze in my tracks when I saw that David Amram was one of Bob's table guests. I almost laughed out loud. While the photographers had gone crazy in their efforts to capture as many shots of Bob Dylan as possible, none of them had realized that one of the most important composers of the twentieth century was sitting right next to him. Before the night was over, I managed to chat briefly with David about one of my favorite books, *Vibrations*, of which he was the author.

Once the show got underway, everything went smoothly. For Dylan's portion of the evening, folk singer Tom Paxton performed "Blowin' In The Wind" and then talked about how Dylan had "changed the landscape" of popular music. When Bob accepted his award, his entire speech consisted of the following sentence: "This is amazing, really, because I never learned to read or write a note of music—and I never will be able to."

I went to bed that night totally exhausted, still wondering why Bob Dylan wanted to have his picture taken with Dinah Shore. When I woke up the next morning, I discovered at least part of the answer. Every morning newscast I saw had a piece about the previous night's awards ceremony, with plenty of shots of Bob and Dinah posing together. Photos of the two of them were in all the papers that day, most of which had the same caption: "The Times They Are a-Changin.'" By the next week, Dylan and Dinah were also in a host of weekly news and gossip magazines. At that point, I determined that Bob Dylan was not only a brilliant singer/songwriter—he was an equally brilliant PR man.

A few months later, I was standing on the wrong side of the backstage fence at the Philadelphia Folk Festival when I spotted David Amram walking toward me. Apparently, for better or worse, I seem to have a face that's hard to forget and a name that's hard to remember. David, being on the backstage side of the fence, reached over the chicken wire to shake hands with me as he said, "Hey, you're the guy from the Songwriters Hall of Fame!"

"Yes, I am," I said. "My name is Randy Poe."

"So, Randy," he said with a big grin on his face, "Did you ever wonder why Bob wanted his picture taken with Dinah Shore that night?"

"Well, Dave, when I saw all the press coverage those photos got, I figured he did it because he knew it'd be on TV and in all the newspapers and magazines."

"That's a good guess," he said. "But the real reason is even better. I saw him posing with her while those photographers were going crazy, stepping all over each other to get shots of the two of them together. So when Bob sat down and the photographers all finally went away, I asked him why on earth he wanted his picture taken with Dinah Shore. He looked at me and he said—dead serious—'So my mother will finally think I'm somebody.'"

~ DON'T BE INTIMIDATED ~

As legendary music icons go, you'd be hard pressed to come up with too many people who go on the list above Bob Dylan. As Tom Paxton said, Dylan "changed the landscape" of popular music. When I met him that night at the Songwriters Hall of Fame dinner, I was in awe, but I didn't stand there speechless—although I don't think anybody would have blamed me if I had. After all, it was Bob Dylan, for Pete's sake!

When it comes to song plugging, you have to be able to face people who are larger than life without turning into a thirteen-year-old fan. Always be respectful, but don't fawn over them. You're not there to worship them. You're there to *help* them. She might already be a superstar, but every singer is looking for another hit. Be impressed with her body of work. Be impressed with how incredible she looks. Be impressed with the fact that her left shoe costs more than everything in your closet combined. But whatever you do, don't be intimidated.

CHAPTER SEVENTEEN

I n 1983, the board of directors of the National Academy of Popular Music/Songwriters Hall of Fame decided—primarily due to the huge success of his *Stardust* album—that Willie Nelson should receive the Academy's Lifetime Achievement Award for his popularity as a performer. Nobody in the organization but me seemed to be aware that Willie was one of the greatest country songwriters of all time.

He'd been on the scene since the early 1960s, writing hits such as "Crazy" for Patsy Cline, "Night Life" for Ray Price, "Hello Walls" for Faron Young, and many other songs that were recorded by the biggest country acts of the day. Between 1962 and 1974, Nelson recorded solo albums for Liberty, RCA, and Atlantic—but the general public wasn't ready to make a star of Willie Nelson, the singer, quite yet.

Finally in 1975, after moving to Columbia Records, Willie singlehandedly changed the face of country music with his sparse, stark, and brilliant concept album, *Red Headed Stranger*. Using his own band, and recording the album in a Texas studio (as opposed to recording in Nashville and being forced to use the same studio musicians every other country artist used, as had been the case during his RCA days), Willie sparked the whole "outlaw" movement, making country music hip enough for the hippies of the day while still keeping the rednecks happy. It was a monumental achievement that would soon turn him into a superstar. It would also cause other country acts to finally have the chance to break away from the cookie-cutter method of recording that the old-line Nashville guard had demanded for decades.

Willie Nelson didn't wear rhinestone suits and cowboy boots. He wore

*Red Headed
Stranger—
Willie
Nelson's
masterpiece.*

jeans, a T-shirt, and sneakers. Instead of a cowboy hat, he wore a bandana. Unlike 98 percent of the country acts before him, there were no fiddlers or steel guitar players in his band. On top of everything else, he not only had a beard, he had the longest hair in country music this side of Crystal Gayle. Willie had been trying to fit in since the early 1960s, but it wasn't until he freed himself from practically every last country cliché that he finally achieved the kind of success that would take him to the very top of the country music world.

Three years after *Red Headed Stranger*, Willie hit on another stroke of genius when he recorded the *Stardust* album—a collection of songs that were far removed from country music. The ten tracks on the record were classics primarily from the 1930s and 1940s, including "All of Me," "Blue Skies," "Georgia On My Mind," and—lo and behold—"September Song," the very song to which Sinatra would later compare "The Girls I Never Kissed."

Most of the men and women who made up the Hall of Fame's board of directors didn't know one country song from another. But everyone on the board knew "All of Me," "Blues Skies, "Georgia On My Mind," and "September Song," so they chose to honor him as a performer. (To the organization's credit, in 2001 Willie was finally and properly inducted into the Songwriters Hall of Fame.)

CERTIFICAT

THIS CERTIFIE

of _____ County, Okla

one year's work in the _____

organized and supervised by

Oklahoma Agric

at Stillwater, in

Department of

to receive this cer

In testimony where

this _____ da

STATE AGENT AND DIRECTOR

CHAPTER EIGHTEEN

★ ★ ★

The day of the awards dinner, March 7, 1983, I was put in charge of meeting Willie and his then-wife Connie in the lobby of the Waldorf Astoria, taking him to meet the waiting press, and then staying in his general vicinity until it was time for him to play a few songs and accept his award.

The reception room was jammed with journalists, photographers, and invited guests. As soon as Willie, Connie, my fiancée Mina, and I walked into the room, the cameras started clicking, and the journalists tossed a few

With Willie Nelson at the 1983 Songwriters Hall of Fame Awards.

questions Willie's way. Unlike the Dylan/Dinah frenzy of the previous year, Willie's Zen-like, mellow demeanor seemed to cast a shroud of calmness over the photographers. I was more than a little relieved. Sam Teicher, the ever-present Hall of Fame photographer, took several shots of Willie and me. Sam's handiwork that night would result in the first of the Willie photos on my office's Wall of Fame.

After the din finally died down, I led Willie and his wife to the Green Room. (There are a lot of Green Rooms in the entertainment business. So far I've never been in one that was actually painted green.) It was the first opportunity for the two of us to have an actual conversation. "Randy," he said, "What songs would you like me to do tonight?"

I was floored. In all the madness leading up to the big night, it was a discussion that had never even been broached in all of my conversations with Willie's manager. It was less than an hour before Willie Nelson would be stepping onto a stage in front of a thousand formally attired people when it suddenly struck me: does he actually perform any of the songs from the *Stardust* album in his concerts?

"Well, Willie, uh, most of the folks in the audience tonight are probably between sixty and eighty years old. So, well, I was kind of hoping you'd do some of the songs from the *Stardust* album—if that's okay with you."

"I'd be happy to," he said. (Clearly, Willie saw the look of relief on my face. Later that evening, he introduced me to one of his associates, saying, "This is Randy. He's the resident worrier for the Songwriters Hall of Fame." For a moment I considered changing the title on my business cards. "Resident worrier" was certainly more apt than "executive director.")

As the cocktail hour party continued nearby, Sam the photographer walked into the Green Room, bringing Gerald Marks and Mitchell Parish with him. Since I knew them both well, I did the introductions. "Willie, this is Gerald Marks. He's the composer of 'All of Me.' And this is Mitchell Parish, who wrote the lyrics to 'Stardust.'"

As Willie shook hands with each of them, Sam went to work, pushing the four of us shoulder to shoulder. While the camera clicked away, the three men exchanged pleasantries—Gerald and Mitchell both expressing their gratitude to

(L–R) Me, Gerald Marks, Willie Nelson, and Mitchell Parish.

Willie for recording their songs. Although no one came right out and said it, by 1983 the album had already sold 3 million copies, contributing mightily to both songwriters' retirement funds.

The resultant photograph, left to right, was yours truly, Gerald, Willie, and Mitchell. Years later I would spot a framed copy of the photo hanging on the wall at the New York Friars Club. There they were: Gerald, Willie, and Mitchell. Someone had done an excellent job of cropping me completely out of the picture. (From that moment on, I always made sure to stand *next* to the famous person when group photos were being taken.)

The emcee for the Songwriters Hall of Fame dinner that year was Dick Clark. Between the various performances and awards presentations, Dick did his usual shtick, keeping the crowd entertained while they waited for the next act to hit the stage.

Everything was going according to plan. The songwriters who were being inducted into the Hall of Fame had all shown up. None of the performers was throwing a temper tantrum. The backing musicians were all on time and in tune. All was right with the world. Then, as Teresa Brewer went on stage to perform "Music! Music! Music!" for what must have been at least the millionth time,

~ THE ANSWER IS "YES" ~

One of the people I admire most in this business is a multitalented gentleman named Rupert Holmes. He wrote and performed the No. 1 hit "Escape (The Piña Colada Song)," won a Tony Award for both the book and score of his musical *Drood*, and created and wrote all fifty-six episodes of the TV show *Remember WENN*. As if that weren't enough, he wrote several more successful musicals, a few novels, and an impressive array of songs that have been recorded by everyone from Barbra Streisand to Britney Spears.

I once had the opportunity to talk to Rupert at length. When I asked him what the secret was to all of his success, his response was, "I said 'yes' to everything anyone in this business asked me to do." It's been a long time since I last spoke to Rupert. Hopefully, he ultimately had a chance to say "no" at least once. But judging from his incredibly prolific body of work, maybe he's still saying "yes" to everybody.

When the theatrical producer Joseph Papp suggested to Rupert that he try his hand at writing a musical, it might have seemed an odd suggestion to a singer/songwriter with no track record in the world of theatre—but Rupert said "yes." Since that day, he's written over a dozen musicals, and now he has a collection of Tony and Drama Desk awards that would have made Joseph Papp very proud.

If you're just beginning the journey of trying to get your songs placed, should an opportunity arise for which you're given the choice to answer either "yes" or "no," remember the words of the extremely successful Rupert Holmes.

Willie's road manager appeared in the Green Room, looking none too happy and coming straight toward me at a pretty rapid clip for a man his size. His name was Randall "Poodie" Locke. He had long hair in a single braided ponytail down his back. He was at least six inches taller than I, and he was massive. Years later I would read a joke on Willie's website: "Question: Why does Poodie wear XXXL T-shirts? Answer: Because he likes 'em tight." I laughed when I read the joke, but back in March of 1983, as Poodie loomed over me, I was feeling pretty somber. Poking an accusatory index finger into my rental-tuxedoed chest, he said, "Somebody shifted all of our gear around backstage. We're going to need at least five minutes to set up once that chick's done singing."

He might as well have said it would take an hour and a half. I headed out the door and across the back of the ballroom, watching as Dick Clark stood just offstage, serenely tapping his foot while Teresa sang. I sidled up next to him and said, "Mr. Clark?"

"Yes?" he said. He was wearing that charming Dick Clark smile—

such a happy-looking man.

"I'm sorry to have to tell you this, but Willie's crew is going to need five minutes to set up after Ms. Brewer finishes singing."

His reaction was slightly worse than I'd expected: Dick Clark—Mr. *American Bandstand*, Mr. Cool, Mr. World's Oldest Teenager—literally dropped to his knees. With his hands clasped together, he looked up at me and whispered, "*Please* tell me you didn't just say 'five minutes.'"

"Yes sir. Five minutes." I grabbed his elbow and pulled him back up. By the time he was standing again, he had managed to regain most of his composure.

"Okay," he said, "Quick as you can, tell me everything you know about Willie Nelson."

I spat out the whole "outlaw" movement thing; that *Red Headed Stranger* was Willie's breakthrough album; that the album's single, "Blues Eyes Crying in the Rain," had gone to No. 1 on the country charts; that *Stardust* was Willie's biggest-selling album to date; that "Always On My Mind" had been his biggest hit single; that I was sure he must've won some Grammy awards and some CMA awards—and suddenly I realized that Teresa Brewer had finished singing and was walking off the stage.

As the applause died down, I stepped to one side. Dick Clark jumped back to his podium as the curtain closed behind him. He started by telling a couple of funny *American Bandstand* stories, and then—just as he began regurgitating everything I had told him about Willie—a noise akin to fifty jackhammers drilling through concrete kicked in behind the curtain. Dick flinched momentarily but plowed on ahead—bestowing more honors, awards, and multimillion-selling records on Willie Nelson by the second.

Through the sound of speaker cabinets scraping across the stage floor, microphone feedback, and other loud, unidentifiable noises, I heard a distinct, "Pssst! Randy!"

I looked to my left and saw Willie in the darkness, behind the curtain, his hand motioning for me to join him onstage. I flew up the steps two at a time. "What can I do for you, Willie?" I whispered.

"Would it be all right with you if we open with 'Whiskey River?'" he asked. His calm demeanor fascinated me as total chaos was going on directly behind

Jody Payne and Willie Nelson performing "Whiskey River."

him. I'd once read an interview with Kris Kristofferson in which he'd said, "Being around Willie is like being around Buddha." Now I understood exactly what he meant.

With Willie talking in one ear and Dick Clark talking about Willie selling more records than Elvis and the Beatles combined in the other, all I could muster was a weak, "Pardon me?"

"'Whiskey River.' We always start our shows with 'Whiskey River.' Would that be all right with you?"

As Willie's words sunk in, I envisioned hundreds of blue-haired ladies fainting dead away while their elderly husbands fell to the floor, clasping their chests as the entire audience breathed its collective final breath.

"It's our tune-up song." Willie said.

"Your what?"

"Our tune-up song. We tune up our instruments while we're doing 'Whiskey River.' If we start with anything else, our guitars and stuff'll be out of tune."

"Of course you can open with 'Whiskey River,'" I said. "How could I possibly say no to Willie Nelson?"

CHAPTER NINETEEN

★ ☆ ★

Like I said earlier, I'm first and foremost a lover of songs and a fan of songwriters, so having a job at the Songwriters Hall of Fame and getting to meet and briefly hang with Bob Dylan and Willie Nelson was a big thrill for me. But Willie and Bob were only two of many I had the opportunity to meet in those days. In fact, thanks to the Hall of Fame, I got to know (or at the very least, shake hands with) some of the greatest songwriters and recording artists of all time. Among them were Smokey Robinson, Neil Diamond, Liza Minnelli, Marvin Hamlisch, Cy Coleman, Chuck Berry, Jimmy Webb, Rosemary Clooney, James Brown, Benny Goodman, and Henry Mancini, as well as the songwriting teams of Gerry Goffin and Carole King, Barry Mann and Cynthia Weil, Alan and Marilyn Bergman, and Jerry Leiber and Mike Stoller. Granted I wasn't making much money, but I was having more fun than a fat billionaire buying a chain of candy stores.

★ ★ ★ ★ ★

The president of the Songwriters Hall of Fame, Sammy Cahn (the man who stuck his head in my office to announce my promotion to executive director by pointing at me and saying, "Okay, Poe, you're it") was one of America's most talented and successful lyricists. Leiber and Stoller were happy to have Sinatra record one of their songs. Frank had recorded entire albums of Sammy's.

Like Leiber and Stoller, Sammy Cahn is not the household name he

Frank Sinatra Sings the Select Sammy Cahn.

should be, but you've certainly heard his songs. For starters, Sammy received more than two dozen Academy Award nominations. He ended up winning four Oscars, and Frank was the one singing three of them. In 1955, Cahn won an Emmy award for "Love and Marriage" (also originally recorded by Sinatra)—a number that would later become the theme song for the TV show *Married . . . with Children.*

Sammy once told me, "From the very beginning, the fates were on my side." The fates initially sided with Sammy by causing a boy named Lou Levy to live around the corner from him on the Lower East Side of Manhattan when the two were still kids in knee pants.

A few years later, in 1933, Sammy would sign his first publishing contract for a song called "Shake Your Head from Side to Side." The publisher's office was in the Roseland Building, which also housed the famous Roseland Ballroom. That same year, Lou Levy was busy winning dance contests at the Roseland. When Sammy bumped into Lou in the hallway of the Roseland Building the day Sammy signed his first publishing contract, Lou asked his old friend what he was doing there. When Sammy told him about the publishing deal, Lou was stunned to discover his childhood pal had become a songwriter. Lou Levy—despite having no visible means of support except his frequent dance contest winnings of a few bucks a week—immediately suggested they should go into business together.

Soon afterward, Sammy Cahn; Sammy's first songwriting partner, Saul Chaplin; and Lou Levy created a publishing company called Leeds Music. Sammy and Saul wrote the songs; Lou plugged them.

When Cahn and Chaplin came up with a song called "Shoe Shine Boy" in 1935, Lou Levy jumped into action. "The building at 729 Seventh Avenue in Manhattan was filled with talent agencies and record companies in those days," Lou once told me. "I gave the elevator operator fifty cents a day to sing 'Shoe Shine Boy' as he went up and down in the car. His passengers would ask him about it and he'd say, 'Oh, that song is gonna be a big hit! You oughta get on it right away!'" By 1936, the artists who had decided to "get on it" included Louis Armstrong, the Mills Brothers, Bing Crosby, Louis Prima, Count Basie, and Duke Ellington. Once word got out about Lou's unique song plugging tactic, one can only imagine how many elevator operators in Manhattan were soon enlisted to start singing other song pluggers' tunes.

~THINK OUTSIDE THE BOX~

Hey, you knew it was coming sooner or later. I hate that phrase too, but some suggestions can't be avoided—especially when it comes to song plugging.

The beauty of pitching songs is that there's not a specific set of guidelines to follow. As a music publisher, I've had songwriters use all sorts of methods to try to get me to listen to their songs.

One day many years ago, I looked up from my desk and saw a young man milling around in the foyer of the company where I was employed at the time. He was wearing a yellow reflector vest, a white hardhat, and a tool belt. The tool belt included one of those electronic gadgets that looks like a glorified phone receiver.

"Can I help you?" I asked as I stepped out of my office.

"I'm from the phone company," he said. "I was told you're having a problem with your phones."

I looked through the open door of the office of one of my coworkers and saw that she was talking away on her phone. So were half the other people in the office suite, including the receptionist.

"I think you're either on the wrong floor or in the wrong building, because we're clearly not having phone problems here."

"Are you Randy Poe?" he asked.

There are certain moments in life that can be pretty disconcerting. For me, this was one of those moments. Looking back on it now, I wish I'd been hip enough to give him my best Clint Eastwood squinty glare while I growled, "That depends on who's asking." Instead, all I could muster was a meek, "Yes."

At that point he reached into a leather pouch on his tool belt. I took about three steps back, desperately trying to remember what terrible offense I'd committed with AT&T, when I saw him pull a cassette tape out of the pouch.

He actually looked a bit sheepish as he handed it to me. "Mr. Poe, I'm not really from the phone company. I just couldn't think of any other way to get my songs to you. I hope you'll listen to them and let me know what you think."

I took the cassette from his hand, smiled a bit sheepishly myself, and said, "I'll be glad to give them a listen. But first, I just might have to go home and change my underwear."

Posing as a phone repairperson isn't necessarily an idea you should jump at, but it was pretty creative—as was Lou Levy's idea of song plugging via elevator operator.

If you can't get your foot in the door subtly, then go ahead and make a splash. Just try not to do anything that'll make everyone in the music business think you're a nutcase—like, say, flying all the way across Canada to pitch a song . . .

CHAPTER TWENTY

★ ✪ ★

Seven months after the 1983 Songwriters Hall of Fame dinner, my best friend Roger Deitz and I went to the BMI country music awards in Nashville, which in those days was held under a massive tent on Music Row—the section of town where most of the music industry is based. Roger's tuxedo was from another decade, if not another century. Mine was a rental, as usual. At least Roger owned his.

We checked in at the entrance, were given little cards with the number of the table we were assigned to, and headed under the "big top." The very first person I bumped into was Willie's manager, Mark Rothbaum. While Roger scouted the room in search of our table, Mark brought me over to Willie's table to say hello to him (personal encounter number 2), and to two of Willie's table mates for the evening, Kris Kristofferson and David Allan Coe.

Later that evening, Roger, Willie, and I ended up in the men's room at the same time. In one of the more awkward introductions I've ever had to make, I said, "Willie, I want you to meet my friend, Roger Deitz." As they both stood there, staring at each other a couple of urinals apart, Roger finally broke the silence with, "I'm really pleased to meet you, and I hope you'll forgive me if I don't shake hands with you right this second."

As the night wore on, with endless awards being handed out to songwriters and music publishers, I noticed that Roger Miller was now also sitting with Willie and his pals.

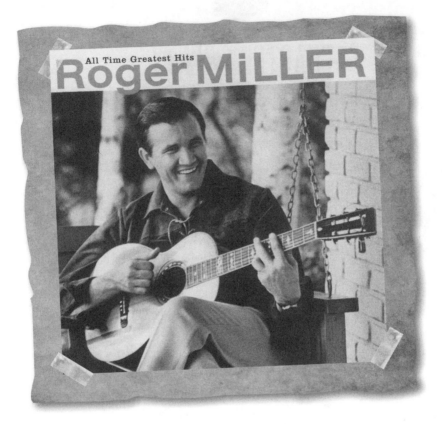

To me, Roger Miller was a legend. I knew more about him than I knew about Willie. He was not only an incredibly talented songwriter, but had also been one of the biggest recording acts of the 1960s, both in the country and pop fields. In 1966–67, he'd even had his own TV show on NBC. Throughout the 1960s, he had written and recorded a long string of hits: "King of the Road," "Dang Me," "Engine, Engine #9," "You Can't Roller Skate in a Buffalo Herd," "England Swings," and many more. He was also the first to record Kristofferson's classic "Me and Bobby McGee" (and Kris didn't even have to land a helicopter on his lawn to get him to cut it).

But in the early 1970s, the public seemed to lose interest. Miller continued to make records for a while, but the days of the big hits as a recording artist

Roger Miller roared back onto the scene in 1985 with *Big River*—a Broadway musical that ran for over 1,000 performances, racking up seven Tony Awards and eight Drama Desk Awards along the way.

were over. In 1978, he simply stopped writing altogether, and by 1983—as far as the record-buying public was concerned—Miller was a has-been. Luckily for Roger Miller, the creative juices would eventually start flowing again. In 1985 he became the king of Broadway with his Tony Award–winning show *Big River*, a musical adaptation of Mark Twain's *Adventures of Huckleberry Finn*. But on this particular October night in 1983, had he not been sitting at the same table with Willie, Kris, and Coe, he could've been easily mistaken for just another one of Nashville's Lower Broadway bums. It was obvious he hadn't shaved for at least a week. But this wasn't Don Johnson/*Miami Vice* stubble. This was "that looks like a homeless guy in a really nice tux" stubble.

At the end of the evening, Roger Deitz and I had nothing better to do than

~AGE AIN'T NOTHING BUT A NUMBER~

Anyone looking at Roger Miller the night he shook my hand would've never dreamed that there was another wave of success heading Miller's way. After all, the track record for most country stars is a series of hits that—sooner or later—comes to an end. Once country radio stops playing your records, you inevitably get dropped by your label. From that point on, you might end up in Branson, you might get to occasionally play the Grand Ole Opry, or you might just tour endlessly until you retire or die. Pleasant isn't it? Welcome to the love and warmth of the country music industry. But I digress . . .

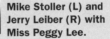

Mike Stoller (L) and
Jerry Leiber (R) with
Miss Peggy Lee.

As a songwriter and/or song plugger, you should never let an artist's age or lack of recent chart action deter you from pitching a song to him or her. If the song is a perfect match for an act that hasn't had a hit since 1995, who cares? Pitch the tune! You never know what might happen: a movie use, a TV show use, or maybe that old-timer's recording of your song could end up being heard by a current star who covers it and turns it into a hit. Or if that old-timer's recording is really outstanding, he might end up having the comeback hit every old-timer dreams of.

Peggy Lee's recording of "Is That All There Is?" is a perfect example of why an artist's age or lack of recent chart action should never be a factor when pitching tunes. By the end of the 1960s, Peggy hadn't had a Top 40 pop hit in over a decade. Luckily, in those days Capitol Records wasn't in the habit of dropping artists as soon as their last single fell off the charts. Peggy Lee was a star in the old-fashioned sense of the word. She didn't have a lot of chart action, but she continued to record albums that sold well, she appeared on a

lot of TV variety shows, and she kept up a respectable concert schedule.

When Miss Lee opened at the Copa in Manhattan, Jerry Leiber went to the show with a demo of "Is That All There Is?" in hand. At the after-party, he gave Peggy the demo and told her what any plugger should say: "This song is right for you." A few days later, she called Jerry to say, "This is my song. This is the story of my life."

After Peggy recorded "Is That All There Is?" she found out that Capitol Records not only didn't plan to release it as a single—the label didn't *want* to release it as a single. Why bother? Her last charting 45 had died at No. 93 four years earlier.

But Peggy Lee was determined to have her way. Shortly after she found out that Capitol didn't intend to put out a single of the very song that she felt was the story of her life, the label tried to book some of its younger acts (hell, they were *all* younger than Peggy Lee) to appear on a late-night television show hosted by Joey Bishop. Joey—an old-timer himself—said he'd only book them if he could also get Peggy Lee. When Peggy heard the news, she agreed to go on Joey's show only if Capitol would release "Is That All There Is?" as a single. Pretty smart move for an old-timer, wouldn't you say?

In 1969, "Is That All There Is?" became the first Top 40 pop hit for Peggy Lee since her recording of "Fever" in 1958! If the song matches the artist, never let age or the length of time since that last hit stop you from making the pitch.

stand under the tent and watch the stars file out. In what remains near the very top of my most bizarre/hysterical/tragic moments in the music business, I noticed that Willie and his entourage were walking straight toward me. Mark the manager came up first, shook my hand, and said, "Goodnight, Randy." Willie was next—a handshake, a big smile (as always), and "Goodnight, Randy." Behind him was Kris Kristofferson, who also shook my hand and, in that wonderful gravely voice of his, said, "'Night, Randy." Even the freakish David Allan Coe nodded his head in my direction as he walked by.

And there stood Roger Miller, looking at me as if I was surely the savior he'd been seeking during his decade in the wilderness. He grabbed my hand—with both of his—and said, "Hello, Randy. Roger Miller. I've been wanting to meet you for the longest time." And he wouldn't let go of my hand. A simple "goodnight" from Mark, Willie, Kris, and David had caused poor Roger Miller to mistake me—a twenty-something-year-old nobody making the kind of salary one makes at a nonprofit organization—for some bigwig music mogul who just might be the very guy to pull him out of the abyss of his oblivion. I smiled, told him it was a pleasure to meet him too, and tried to look like the most successful man in the room—in my ill-fitting rented tuxedo and dark brown loafers. On that October night in 1983, no one could have predicted that there would be better days ahead for both of us.

CHAPTER TWENTY-ONE

When an unexpected opportunity came my way in the mid-1980s, I decided the time had come to leave my position at the Songwriters Hall of Fame. Sid Bernstein—the renowned agent responsible for bringing the Beatles to America for the first time in 1964 (and later the Rolling Stones, the Kinks, the Moody Blues, and others)—had asked me to join him in a new independent record label he had just been hired to run.

The idea was for Sid to oversee the label and for me to set up and run the company's music publishing division. The backers of this venture had deep enough pockets to make the offer too good for me to turn down. (By now I was married and felt I had lived paycheck to paycheck long enough.) To my pleasant surprise, shortly after I resigned from my position at the Songwriters Hall of Fame, I was elected to its board of directors, giving me the opportunity to continue to be involved with the organization long after I had ceased to be employed there.

Unfortunately for Sid's new indie label (and for me), the 1980s turned out to be the decade when the major record labels (Columbia, Warner Bros., RCA, EMI, and the rest) absolutely took over the industry. Until then, independent record labels still had a chance to score the occasional hit single. But thanks to the major labels' willingness to spend a fortune on "promotional expenses," it became virtually impossible for the smaller labels to compete.*

In addition, once MTV came along, there was suddenly no reason to put out a single if you weren't going to also put out a corresponding video. So along with the cost of pressing records and paying promotion men exorbitant fees to get radio stations to pay attention to your latest single, you had the extra expense of making, essentially, a small motion picture to go along with every release.

So as Sid's record label was busy losing vast sums of money in salaries, manufacturing costs, and moviemaking, I sat in my office down the hall, signing songwriters.

The very first person I signed, Brian Slawson, was an artist who created uniquely original works based on various pieces of classical music. We entered into a publishing agreement for all of the compositions on his first album that was just about to be released on Columbia Records. I was very proud of Brian when his debut album resulted in his Grammy nomination for "Best New *Classical* Artist" the following year, but by that time, I had already left to go to work for Leiber and Stoller.

....
* To get the complete behind-the-scenes story about promotion men and the whole sordid record business of the 1980s, read *Hit Men: Power Brokers and Fast Money Inside the Music Business* by Fredric Dannen.

Although my stay at Sid's company didn't last long, it did provide me with the very first Nashville song plugging experience of my career. Decades later, I can safely say I've never had another one like it—and I'm sure I never will.

As odd as it might seem, I had found a small pocket of country songwriters right in the middle of New York City. Since I'd been a country disc jockey in Alabama at one point during my brief radio career, I was pretty familiar with the genre. Plus, I knew a good country song when I heard one, so I began entering into publishing agreements with some of the writers I'd discovered in Manhattan.

Having gotten to meet a lot of industry people when Roger Deitz and I had gone to Nashville in 1983, I started calling my contacts there, setting up appointments. By the time I arrived in Nashville with my briefcase full of country cassettes, I had meetings scheduled with several top country record producers and a few A&R folks from various major record labels.

The standard procedure in those pre–compact disc days was to put the demo of each song you were plugging onto an individual cassette tape. That way, if a producer wasn't interested in what he was hearing on one tape, he would just pop it out of the machine and you'd hand him the next one. There was no time to fast-forward in search of the next song.

If a record producer or an A&R person really liked what he was hearing, he would tell the song plugger that he wanted to put a "hold" on the song. (The definition of a "hold" requires a quick explanation of another facet of US copyright law: If a song has already been recorded and commercially released, anyone can then record that same song, as long as mechanical royalties are properly paid to the copyright owner. If a song has *never* been recorded and commercially released, the copyright owner is the sole party who can grant an artist the right to record that specific song. When a record producer, for example, says he wants to put a "hold" on a particular song, that means he wants you to refrain from playing that song for anyone else, because he wants to have the chance for an artist he's producing to be the first to record and release the song in question. Nobody wants to spend a fortune on session musicians and studio time recording a "new" song, only to discover that the song he or she has just recorded is about to be released on another label by another act.)

One other point of note: Putting a "hold" on a song is not a guarantee that the song will be recorded. Usually a "hold" is for a very finite period of time. If the artist doesn't like the song, it's no longer on hold. If the artist finishes recording an album and doesn't record the song, it's generally no longer on hold. It's the song plugger's job to stay in touch with the producer, manager, A&R person at the label, etc., to find out whether or not a song is still on hold.

My very first meeting in Nashville was with the head of A&R at one of the biggest labels in town. Since he's still alive and in the business, I won't use his real name. Let's just call him Larry. Larry had a gorgeous office and the finest audio equipment I'd ever seen. We said hello and went straight to work. I handed him the first cassette. He slid it into the machine and the demo began to play. To me, the song had never sounded better—probably because I'd never heard it played through such great speakers. But Larry loved it too. I kept waiting for him to hit the stop button and ask to hear the next song. Instead, he listened to it from start to finish, and when the song ended, he looked at me and said, "That's a great song! I want to put a hold on that one."

My first Nashville song plugging trip, my first meeting, my first song—and one of the most powerful record guys on Music Row wanted to hold it for one of his artists. I sat there thinking, "Nobody is this lucky."

The next cassette I handed to Larry was a duet—and this time he was knocked out again. He told me he wanted to keep that one too, because the bestselling female country star on his label had just scored a major duet hit with a new male pop act on the label. Larry told me, "We're looking for a follow-up right now—and this song just might be it."

I handed him another cassette. This one was my "ace in the hole" because my writer had cowritten the song with a Major Pop Star, and the Major Pop Star had done my writer a solid by recording the lead vocal for the demo. Larry was more than a little impressed. Before the song had even ended, he was already telling me who he thought it would be right for at his label. I just kept sitting there thinking to myself, "It can't be this easy."

I left Larry's office with three holds, walking on air. As time passed, I would come to discover I was right about two things: nobody is that lucky, and it really *can't* be that easy. I followed up with Larry time and time again over the next several months, and every time I called, he'd practically beg me to let him hang on to those three songs just a little bit longer. Years later I would learn from several others who had suffered the same fate that Larry asked for a hold on virtually *everything* he listened to. Perhaps he was worried he might accidentally let a huge hit slip through his fingers—or perhaps he already had, and didn't want to ever let it happen again.

Thanks to the generous help of Del Bryant—who was then working at BMI's Nashville office (and who would eventually become President and CEO of the organization)—I also got to meet with some of Music Row's hottest record producers that week. It was all very enjoyable and educational until the final day of the trip.

My very last meeting in Nashville was with a man who had produced several No. 1 country records. Despite all of his success, his office was in a basement. I could only surmise that this was by his own choice, since he had not only produced a number of hits, he had also written songs recorded by some of country's bestselling artists. On top of that, he was also a successful music publisher. He could've been renting a penthouse office if he chose to, but he'd gone the other direction.

When I finally found the door to the basement, I had to knock hard because there was no doorbell. Apparently there was no personal assistant either. The producer answered the door himself and invited me in. As I was sitting down, he said the following: "Del tells me you're from New York City." It was said in the exact same tone he would have used if the sentence had been, "Del tells me you're a serial rapist."

I was a tad surprised by his accusatory tone, but by this time I'd been in the music business way too long to let anyone intimidate me. (Being a rejection-based industry, the music business is not—and has never been—for the overly sensitive. As country songwriter Bob Morrison once said, "In Nashville you need the heart of a poet and the hide of a rhino.")

"Well, actually I'm from Muscle Shoals, Alabama," I told him.

"But you live in New York City now," he said.

"That's right."

"Okay, let's hear what you've brought."

I pulled out a cassette and handed it to him. He put it in his machine, hit

~ DO YOUR HOMEWORK ~

Most of us stumble through life learning lessons the hard way. It's human nature to do so, and one might argue that it's for the best. On the other hand, for me it has occasionally ended up resulting in broken bones and other unpleasantness. When it comes to song plugging, it never hurts to have a little advance notice of what's on the other side of that proverbial basement door.

If you are about to interact with someone in the music business for the first time, learn as much as possible about that person in advance. From the biggest superstar to the office-building doorman, the music world is filled with eccentric characters.

I once produced a demo of a song using a small backing band and a male vocalist. I thought the song would be great for a specific vocal group until I spoke to someone else who had pitched a song to the same act. "Believe it or not," he told me, "if you want them to cut one of your songs, you've got to make a four-part harmony demo, because otherwise they can't figure out their parts."

One of the reasons I keep stressing the importance of getting to know everyone you can in the business is so you can ask the people you know about someone you've yet to meet. There's nothing worse than showing up at a meeting dressed like Hercule Poirot, only to find out the person you're meeting has a thing against bow ties. When it comes to song plugging, remember what your parents and teachers always told you: do your homework.

the "Play" button, and then hit the "Stop" button before the brief introduction was even over.

He looked off into the distance—as if I wasn't in the room—and said, "I don't see how nobody from New York City can have a gawddamn *clue* about what a good country song is."

I took a deep breath. "Well, like I said, I'm not *from* New York. I'm from Alabama."

He took the cassette out of the machine and said, "What else you got?"

I handed him another tape. As he was putting it in his cassette player, the basement door flew open, and in walked a Major Country Star. The producer stood up and said, "Hey man, how are ya? This here's Randy Poe. He thinks he knows country music, but he's from New York City. Do you b'*lieve* this shit?"

The Major Country Star just smiled and shook my hand—at which point I realized his eyes were like spinning pinwheels. He was a minimum of four sheets to the wind, and it wasn't even noon. But he was still coherent enough to drawl, "Are you really from New York City?"

"No, I'm not. I'm from Muscle Shoals, Alabama, which means when I was a disc jockey spinning your records on the radio down there, I was further south than either one of you are right now."

They both looked stumped for a moment, and then a siren began to wail in the distance. When it became obvious that the siren was getting closer, the record producer and the Major Country Star literally ran to the basement window—which, of course, was up near the room's ceiling. I sat back down, waiting for it to pass, as I watched two grown men standing on their tiptoes in cowboy boots, craning their necks in an effort to see the approaching emergency vehicle.

The millisecond it was parallel with the building, the only thing that could be seen were the wheels flying past at high speed. And then the record producer spoke again. He turned to the Major Country Star, and with a look of total disgust on his face, jerked his head in my direction as he said, "I guess a *city* boy don't get excited when a *am*-bew-lance goes by."

I stood up, popped the cassette out of the tape deck, and headed for the basement door.

The time would eventually come—after I'd been with Leiber and Stoller for a few years—when we would have No. 1 singles on the country charts with Randy Travis, Alan Jackson, and LeAnn Rimes, as well as recordings of our songs on hit albums by dozens of other country acts.

The night I was on network television, accepting an Academy of Country Music award as copublisher of the "Song of the Year," the producer who called me a city slicker and the Major Country Star were nowhere to be seen.

Last I heard, the producer was critiquing songs by amateur songwriters over the Internet for a fee. The Major Country Star died tragically young, less than five years after the day the *am*-bew-lance went by.

CHAPTER TWENTY-TWO

★ ★ ★

Throughout my years in the music business, I've been accused by many of being just plain old lucky. I can't argue with the accusation, because it's true. But just like all those other clichés we've already covered, there's another one that I keep in mind every day: sometimes you make your own luck.

Here's an example: When I was still at the Songwriters Hall of Fame, I got a call from Bill Boggs. Bill would later go on to win four Emmy awards, appear in motion pictures and network television shows, write a bestselling book, and be very successful in many other entertainment field endeavors. Back in the 1980s, he was a local midday talk-show host for a television station in Manhattan. He had called to say he needed me to help round up some songwriters for his show. I got on the phone and called up Sammy Cahn (for obvious reasons), George David Weiss (whose hits included "Can't Help Falling in Love," "What a Wonderful World," and "The Lion Sleeps Tonight"), and Jerry Leiber and Mike Stoller—a songwriting team I'd admired from the time I was a kid because they'd written the two earliest songs in my conscious memory: "Hound Dog" and "Charlie Brown."

Now on the day Bill Boggs did his interview with Sammy, George, Jerry, and Mike, I could have just watched the show on the television set back at my office. But I wanted to be there in person, because I wanted to have the chance to possibly spend some time with Leiber and Stoller. I'd met them both when they'd once come to an event at the Hall of Fame, but I'd never had the chance to tell them how much I appreciated their work. (Right, like they'd never heard that before.)

~MAKE YOUR OWN LUCK~

Making your own luck doesn't mean carrying a four-leaf clover around in one pocket and a rabbit's foot in the other—although it probably couldn't hurt. Making your own luck really means being as proactive as possible. It's about seeking out opportunities instead of waiting for them to come to you.

Going back to my Songwriters Hall of Fame days for a moment, I was lucky that the executive director's job became available so soon after I went to work there. But I made my own luck by getting to know all of the board members within a matter of weeks after I walked in the door. If I hadn't been proactive—if I had decided it might be better to wait a few months before I started spending time with each of the board members individually—my inactions probably would've resulted in someone else getting the gig.

Don't wait for luck to come to you. Anticipate. Plan ahead. Be proactive. Use every opportunity at hand to make your own luck.

I went to the television studio and watched while the four songwriters sat around the table with Bill, spending an hour telling great stories about writing songs recorded by Sinatra, Elvis, the Beatles, Peggy Lee, Dean Martin, Ella Fitzgerald, Louis Armstrong, and other music icons.

When the show ended, everyone left the studio except Jerry and Mike. The two of them remained seated at the interview table, engrossed in conversation with each other. Granted, I was your "standard variety lucky" that they didn't get up and leave when everyone else did; but, consciously or not, I made my own luck when I walked over to the table, pulled up a chair, and interjected myself into their conversation. I wasted no time with small talk. I just started telling them about some of my favorite lesser-known songs of theirs—songs so obscure that they were clearly surprised anyone knew about them. I didn't do it because I was job hunting or looking to "network." I did it because I truly admired their talents as songwriters and record producers, and because I wanted to get to *know* them. We ended up talking for over an hour.

When the three of us were informed that somebody else needed the studio, we wrapped up our conversation and headed our separate ways. After that, outside of seeing them at a Songwriters Hall of Fame dinner the following year, I had very little contact with either Jerry or Mike.

As it turned out, to quote Sammy Cahn, "the fates were on my side." By 1985, Leiber and Stoller had parted ways with their old business partner Freddy Bienstock, and had set up new offices in the Galleria on 57th Street. Meanwhile, I had moved on from the Songwriters Hall of Fame to take the music publishing job at Sid Bernstein's indie record label.

I was sitting in my office one day—well aware that the label was on the verge of collapse—when the receptionist told me Mike Stoller was on the phone. Although we hadn't talked in over a year, he'd obviously remembered me from the day I'd forced my way into the conversation after Bill Boggs's TV show. Word must have gotten out on the street that the company where I was working was about to go the way of the dial telephone. When I said hello, Mike cut right to the chase. "Do you know anybody who might be looking for a job?" he asked.

I cut to the chase too. "You're talking to him," I said.

CHAPTER TWENTY-THREE

★ ✦ ★

My first few months with Leiber and Stoller were spent learning the songs in their publishing company. Along with the songs they wrote, there were thousands more that they had acquired either by signing writers such as Jeff Barry and Ellie Greenwich ("Do Wah Diddy Diddy," "Chapel of Love"), Burt Bacharach and Hal David ("Close to You," "Anyone Who Had a Heart"), and George "Shadow" Morton ("Leader of the Pack"), or by purchasing entire publishing companies that owned copyrights by Bobby Darin, George Jones, Harlan Howard, Buck Owens, Carole Bayer Sager, Melissa Manchester, James Brown, John Sebastian, Stephen Sondheim, and hundreds of others.

During the 1960s and 1970s, Jerry and Mike had acquired a number of these publishing companies in partnership with Freddy Bienstock, a man who had once been a song plugger for Hill and Range Songs. Hill and Range had copublishing agreements with Elvis Presley's music publishing interests: Elvis Presley Music and Gladys Music. Throughout much of Elvis's career, if a songwriter had any hope of getting Elvis to record his or her song, it had to first meet with Freddy's approval.

"I was not enamored with rock & roll at first," Freddy once said in an interview. "But I changed after a while. By listening to the songs that were submitted to me for Elvis, I soon had a good idea of what he wanted. I would take demos to Memphis and have him select the songs he wanted to do at the recording sessions."

Freddy's job was like a double-edged sword. He got credit for being the song plugger who found many of Elvis's hits, but he also had to take the

~KNOW YOUR CATALOG~

A music publisher refers to the entire collection of songs in the company as "the catalog." It's another one of those phrases (like "mechanical device") that used to have a literal meaning in the publishing world. Going all the way back to when song pluggers were still traveling salesmen, the pluggers would keep all of the samples of their sheet music in binders. Later, music publishers created literal catalogs of their hits—usually comprised of the first page or two of the sheet music of each song, so that potential users of the music could get an idea of how the song went. As time passed, the word "catalog" stuck, even though music publishers don't print actual paperbound catalogs anymore.

Much of my song plugging over the years has gone like this: Someone calls me on the phone and says, "[Famous Film Director] is looking to replace [Famous Song Title] for a scene in her movie because [Famous Eccentric Publisher] is quoting too high." What that means in layman's terms is that another publisher has asked for more money to use a song he represents than the film's music budget allows. So the film in question now needs a similar song to replace the overpriced song at a more reasonable fee.

Since I know my catalog, I can suggest a potential replacement almost instantaneously. First I ask if the song being replaced fits the scene in the movie because of the song's subject matter, the song's tempo, or the song's "feel." As soon as I have an answer, I don't have to look through lists. I don't have to wrack my brain. I don't have to ask anyone else. I know my catalog. I also know the sooner I can suggest a substitute song and email an audio file of it to the person on the other end of the line, the better chance I have of getting my song into the movie.

If you're a songwriter and you get word that a film director is looking to replace a specific song, you can either suggest one you've already written or you can get to work writing a new one. Don't infringe on somebody else's copyright, of course. But if the director needs a song about flowers, write your own song about flowers. If he needs a song with a James Brown feel to it, write something funky. If he needs a power ballad—no problem. But before you knock yourself out writing something new, think about everything you've already written. If the demo's already in the can, get it to him a.s.a.p.

Whether you're a songwriter plugging your own songs or a song plugger at a publishing company with hundreds or thousands of songs to promote, know your catalog.

blame for all the ones that tanked.

Along with having a good ear for a good song, Bienstock was an extremely astute businessman. His very first job in the music business was as a fourteen-year-old stock boy at the prestigious music publishing firm of Chappell & Co. Decades later, Freddy would end up *buying* Chappell & Co. He would eventually make millions in profits by selling Chappell & Co. to Warner Bros. Music (which is why the company is now called Warner/Chappell Music, Inc.). Not bad for a former stock boy.

CHAPTER TWENTY-FOUR

★ ✪ ★

By the end of the 1980s, I had spent a decade living in New York, getting to know everyone I possibly could in the music industry there. In January of 1989, Jerry and Mike asked me to meet them for lunch at the Friars Club—the same place Jerry had pitched "The Girls I Never Kissed" to Frank Military three years earlier (and also the same place where the photo of Gerald Marks, Willie Nelson, and Mitchell Parish sans me hung on the wall). It was there on that winter day in 1989 that my bosses announced their desire to move the company (which, at that point, consisted of the two of them and me) to California—immediately.

★ ★ ★ ★ ★

On my very last day in Manhattan, I locked the front door of what was now the former office of Leiber & Stoller Music Publishing and got in my car to drive across the 59th Street Bridge one final time. As I drove toward the bridge, a fellow motorist coming toward me came a tad too close to my car, catching my rear bumper on her rear bumper as she passed by. It was instantly evident that mine was the lighter of the two vehicles, when I felt the strange sensa-

tion of being yanked backward for a split second. I watched helplessly through the rearview mirror as my back bumper ripped free and began doing cartwheels down 59th Street, finally coming to rest on a curb.

It was time. Goodbye, New York. Hello, Hollywood.

CHAPTER TWENTY-FIVE

As excited as I was about moving to Los Angeles, I knew it meant I would have to essentially start over in a lot of ways, because virtually all of my music industry contacts were based in New York and Nashville. I'd be lying if I said I wasn't a little apprehensive about having to shift back into first gear again. After all, I wasn't in my twenties anymore. The one thing I'd failed to take into account though was good old *luck*.

At lunchtime—the very first day in my new office on Sunset Boulevard—I went to the elevator to go in search of food. I had literally moved to town over the weekend and driven to work that Monday morning. When the elevator doors opened, there stood Sammy Cahn.

"Holy shit!" I said, rather unprofessionally. "What are you doing here?"

"What am *I* doing here?" he laughed. "I think the more appropriate question is, 'What are *you* doing here?'"

"We moved the company to the West Coast this past weekend," I told him as I stepped into the elevator. "My new office is on this floor. Are you visiting somebody in this building?"

"Well, not exactly," he told me. "Warner/Chappell's offices are upstairs. I have an office up there, about five floors above you."

In addition to his place in Manhattan, I knew Sammy had a house in Beverly Hills, but I didn't know he had a West Coast office until that moment. And even though I've lived a life filled with an inordinate amount of coincidences, the fact that his office and mine were in the same building came as quite a shock.

"What are you doing right now?" Sammy asked me.

"I'm taking my lunch break. Any place around here you can recommend?"

"There are plenty of restaurants in the neighborhood, but I think we should go to Pink's." (In case you're not familiar with the famed eateries of Los Angeles, Pink's is a hot dog stand on LaBrea Avenue that's been in business since 1939.)

"That sounds good to me," I said.

"Great," said Sammy. "You drive."

So there I was, my first day on the job in LA, having lunch with my old boss from my Songwriters Hall of Fame days in New York. As the months passed, Sammy became my conduit to meeting many, many West Coast music industry folks. The fates had obviously packed up and moved to Los Angeles with me.

CHAPTER TWENTY-SIX

★ ✪ ★

As the years in LA flew by, the company grew at a rapid clip. It wasn't very long before Leiber & Stoller Music Publishing transformed from an entity of three to a company comprised of a staff large enough to take up almost an entire floor of the office building at 9000 Sunset Boulevard.

After years of having outsourced all of the company's administrative duties (royalties, licensing, copyright, and so forth), Jerry, Mike, and I brought everything in-house, putting together a cherry-picked team of very talented music publishing executives and support staff.

As we grew, we signed new writers and continued to acquire other publishing catalogs. It was an exciting time, but as the company expanded, my job began having less to do with music and more to do with personnel and paperwork. I felt trapped in an office instead of being "on the street" in the middle of the action. For me, the days of hanging out in clubs and recording studios had ground to a trickle. I knew I had to either work my way back into the creative end of the business or end up being just another "suit." So I created my own niche that allowed me to get my focus back on the music—which leads us to the next cliché: timing is everything.

Today we live primarily in a digital

music world. While the heads of all the major record labels were asleep at the wheel in the mid-1990s, consumers of music had discovered that audio files could be uploaded, downloaded, and exchanged over the Internet for free. It sounds silly now, but the record companies were still focusing all of their attention on trying to sell physical CDs, while the very audience they most wanted to reach was busy downloading those very labels' recordings without paying for them.

This meant that artists, songwriters, record producers, and everyone else who made a living from record sales were all being robbed blind, thanks primarily to the major record labels' failure to simply keep up with modern technology.

If it weren't for Steve Jobs and his Apple gang creating a legal music downloading service with iTunes, I'm convinced that the music industry would have eventually suffered irreparable damage (and perhaps I'm being overly optimistic to think it hasn't already).

But before the days of iTunes and other digital music services, the popular format for listening to music was the CD; and before that, it was the 33 1/3–rpm long-playing vinyl album, the 45-rpm single, the prerecorded cassette tape, and, for a brief season, this ridiculous cartridge device called an 8-track tape. Even though it wasn't really all that long ago, vinyl albums, singles, cassettes, and (especially) 8-track tapes now seem downright arcane. Lately there's been a resurgence of the vinyl album, but the fact that there's been a resurgence means, by definition, that at one time it was considered passé.

When we moved our company to the West Coast in 1989, vinyl and cassettes were just beginning to be replaced by CDs. I can still remember going to Tower Records on Sunset Boulevard (when there still *was* a Tower Records on Sunset Boulevard), watching the bins slowly being changed out from album-size racks to CD-size racks. In fact, going to Tower Records at lunchtime was pretty much my only escape from the office—but it gave me an idea that would turn out to be a whole new way of plugging the songs in our publishing company.

Music publishers have always looked for ways to make their catalogs available to various users of popular music: advertising agencies, record producers, music supervisors (the men and women who choose the music to be used in movies and TV shows), and anyone else who might need to license songs for various projects. Once the long-playing album came to prominence in the 1950s, the solution was for a publisher to manufacture 33 1/3–rpm vinyl albums comprised primarily of hits from the company's catalog. These albums were not sold in stores. They were used only for promotion. In the 1970s, publishers moved away from vinyl albums and began using prerecorded cassette tapes. Major music publishers and smaller independent publishing companies alike promoted their catalogs via cassette for the next couple of decades.

As soon as I saw that some of the bins at Tower Records were being changed to fit CDs, I knew we needed to jump on the bandwagon immediately. My staff found a company that was willing to manufacture relatively small batches of CDs; my wife, Mina (a graphic designer), created the artwork for the covers; and soon Leiber & Stoller Music Publishing was the first publisher to have a portion of its catalog available on what was then a brand new format.

We started out with just two CDs, consisting of hits written by Jerry and Mike. We sent them to everyone we could think of: record producers, record company executives, movie directors, script writers, TV show producers, recording artists, ad agencies, artist managers, music supervisors—even radio stations.

As it turned out, we got an unexpected response from the program directors at radio stations. They had been desperate for CDs of something besides the current Top 40 hits, because most of the record labels had yet to go back to their older albums and begin reissuing them on CD. Radio stations were dying to be able to switch entirely to CDs so they wouldn't have to deal with 45s anymore. (Although it's fun to take a nostalgic look back at the quaintness of 45-rpm singles, the truth is they were a nightmare for disc jockeys. To play a 45 starting at the exact spot where the music began, you literally had to put the needle down somewhere near where the grooves started and then manually spin the record backwards until the sound stopped. As if that weren't tricky enough, you never knew when a 45 might start skipping—either causing the record to play the same two or three notes over and over or causing the needle to unexpectedly jump over entire sections of a song.)

The two CDs of songs written by Leiber and Stoller got such a positive response within the music community that we decided to ratchet things up several notches by creating a sales tool comprised of many more songs from our catalog—a full-blown boxed set of hits with packaging that would be equal parts elegant and outrageous.

To their credit, Jerry and Mike realized the concept's promotional potential, so no expense was spared. The idea was to come up with a design that would catch everyone's attention, be easy to use, and—with any luck at all—pay for itself with just a couple of song placements in movies, TV shows, or even a single commercial. (The amount a publisher charges for the use of a song in a movie, television show, or commercial is called the synchronization fee. Unlike mechanical royalties that have a set rate, synchronization fees are entirely negotiable. The better known the song, the more a publisher is likely to charge for its use. Getting

~PRESENTATION IS CRUCIAL TO SUCCESS~

As a music publisher, I've been getting songs in the mail for decades. Years ago they arrived via cassette. In more recent years, they've shown up on CDs. And most of them looked as if they were labeled by a grade-schooler.

When you're promoting your songs, you're also promoting yourself. You can write songs in cut-offs and a tank top, but unless you're Daisy Duke, it's not a good idea to pitch them in the same outfit.

Technology keeps making things easier and easier for all of us. When you're preparing to pitch a song, use the technology you have available. If you're burning the song onto a CD, use your computer to print the song title and contact information on the label. Don't write the information on the label or the CD face in your own hand unless you're a calligrapher.

If you are asked to email an audio file by someone, attach a scan of the lyrics. If you have a lead sheet of the song, that's even better. Keep your email message brief and to the point. There's no need to tell the recipient your life story.

I've sat and listened to at least 1,000 wannabe songwriters tell me that their songs are as good as any other songs they've heard in their songwriting course. Every time I've heard that speech, I've given the same response: "You aren't competing against other amateurs. You're competing against songwriters with multiplatinum records on their walls."

The same holds true for novice song pluggers. If you're a first-timer trying to get a major artist to record your song, your competition isn't all of the others out there who haven't had a song recorded before. You're competing with song pluggers who have longstanding track records with multimillion-selling acts.

Be professional. Sound professional. Act professional. Look professional. Of course, the song is the most important element, but presentation is crucial to success.

a song used in a movie or TV show is nice, but the money one can make from a national commercial is often six figures. If a commercial campaign runs for an extended period of time, the income can easily reach seven figures.)

Hysterical debates raged at the office for weeks as everyone tossed in his or her two cents about what the package should look like, which songs should be included, and whether or not to divide the CDs up by genre, year, or some other manner.

As hard as it is to believe today, there were a number of hit records that made their first appearance in the CD format on what became a six-CD boxed set containing 150 of the most important songs in our catalog.

When the arguments finally died down, the CDs were divided up by genre: R&B, country, rock & roll, pop, standards, and Elvis. The binder that held the CDs was covered in gold cloth, and the slipcover the binder slid into was navy blue. The company logo was embossed on both the binder and the slipcover. Like I said, equal parts elegant and outrageous.

No other music publisher had ever done anything like it. As soon as the shipment arrived at our office, we began sending the six-CD promotional packages out to everyone in the entertainment industry that we could find an address for, just as we'd done with the previous two CDs. To say the plan worked would be an understatement. Every single "promo-pack" was its own little song plugger in a box.

We now live in a world where songs are primarily promoted digitally. But to this day, when I visit other music executives, I still frequently see our old six-CD promo-pack in their offices.

CHAPTER TWENTY-SEVEN

While I was busy trying to create new ways to promote songs, my best friend Roger Deitz (he whom I'd introduced to Willie Nelson in the men's room at the BMI country awards over a decade earlier) was busy writing articles for various music magazines. At one point, he did a lengthy interview with Willie that resulted in a cover story on the man and his famous Martin N-20 guitar, Trigger, for a magazine called *Acoustic Guitar*.

Willie dug the article so much that he invited Roger to one of his shows, followed by a post-concert visit to the bus. As they sat at the little table in the bus's galley, Willie opened a bottle of Jack Daniel's, took a swig, and then passed it over to Roger. Roger took a swig of his own and passed it back. Luckily, Roger stayed sober enough to notice a pile of 8" x 10" photos of Willie stacked on the table in front of him. Knowing I was a fan, Roger asked Willie to autograph a photo inscribed to me.

Of course, as soon as it came in the mail, I proudly framed it and hung it next to the photo of Willie and me at the Songwriters Hall of Fame dinner, not realizing that my growing collection of Willie photos would eventually lead to the understandable presumption that Willie and I were pals.

Putting the most popular songs from our catalog on promotional CDs caused me to ponder

the possibility
of convincing record labels to include more of our songs on their commercial releases of compilation CDs. (A compilation CD is an album consisting
of a collection of recordings by various artists, frequently centered on a specific
theme.) Since our catalog included huge hits such as "The Twist," "Under the
Boardwalk," "Jailhouse Rock," "Fever," "I Got You (I Feel Good)," "Kansas

City," and other songs known by practically everyone on the planet, the original hit recordings of most of those songs had already gradually begun to appear on CD. What I wanted to do was become actively involved in the actual creation of compilation CDs. My plan was to come up with compilation ideas that would include songs from our catalog and then pitch those ideas to record labels.

Naturally, this led back to cliché number 1: it's not what you know—it's who you know. I didn't even know if record labels would accept compilation ideas from outside sources. After all, the labels had their own in-house staffs whose jobs were to come up with compilation ideas. Not having answers to any of my questions, I knew I had to get to know the folks who did. Two of the biggest players in the compilation market were Rhino Records and K-tel. Once again, the fates were with me.

There's a Riot Goin' On!—A collection of eighteen hits from the songwriting team of Jerry Leiber and Mike Stoller.

The Muscle Shoals Sound – My CD tribute to the little Alabama town once known as the "Hit Recording Capital of the World."

Just as I was trying to figure out how to introduce myself to the appropriate creative people at Rhino, I got a phone call from someone in the business affairs department of that very label, in need of a favor. Within a week, I was at Rhino's offices, pitching ideas for compilation CDs. My first two concepts were a collection of Leiber and Stoller's hits (using the original recordings by the original artists) and a collection of hits recorded in Muscle Shoals, Alabama. Even though Leiber and Stoller had been writing songs and producing records for over forty years at that point, no label in the US had ever put together an album of their biggest hits. And although there had been dozens of hits recorded in Muscle Shoals, no one had ever put together a compilation of those songs on an album either.

The guys and gals at Rhino Records dug both ideas. My job was to pick the

50 Coastin'
Classics –
A two-CD
compilation
of recordings
by legendary
vocal group,
the Coasters.

specific recordings to be included on the CDs, sequence them (which meant figuring out what order they should go in), and write the liner notes. The release of both CDs resulted in a ton of press, and they even sold quite a few copies. Both of my feet were now in the door. I had found a whole new song plugging niche that very few, if any, music publishers had ever tried before.

The biggest act Leiber and Stoller had produced for Atlantic Records back in the 1950s and early 1960s was the Coasters. Jerry and Mike had written all of the vocal group's hits ("Charlie Brown," "Yakety Yak," "Poison Ivy," "Searchin'," "Along Came Jones," "Young Blood," "Little Egypt," etc.)—all of which we also published. Because I'd shown Rhino that I could put together a couple of compilation CDs, James Austin, one of Rhino's A&R men, called me to ask for help in putting together a Coasters anthology. By the time we were done, it had turned into a two-CD set called *50 Coastin' Classics*.*

With just a little luck, and by following my old college instructor's advice to get to know everyone I could in the music business, I had managed to help put together a package containing around four dozen songs from our publishing company. But things only got better. Two years later, Rhino released a sixteen-song CD called *The Very Best of the Coasters*, using the same liner notes I'd written for *50 Coastin' Classics*. Without any additional work on my part, we'd ended up with a second Coasters release for which we owned all sixteen copyrights.

Around the same time I began putting together compilations for Rhino, I found myself at yet another BMI awards dinner. This time it was the organization's annual pop awards in LA. Just like all those years earlier at the BMI country awards in Nashville, everyone was assigned a table number. I found my table, sat down, and introduced myself to the stranger sitting next to me. He knew who Leiber and Stoller were, but he had no clue who I was. Despite that, his first words to me—before even telling me his name—were, "Do you know anything about country music?"

I said, "You mean like, was I a country disc jockey in Alabama for a couple of years?"

He smiled like a Cheshire cat as he introduced himself. "My name is Owen Husney," he said, "And I'm looking for someone in LA who's an expert on the subject of country music."

"Well, they're hard to find in these parts, but maybe I can help you out. What do you need?"

"I need somebody to put together country compilations for my company."

"What company would that be?" I asked.

"K-tel," he said.

Now it was my turn to smile like a Cheshire cat.

★ ★ ★ ★ ★

....
* In truth, after several months, James Austin and I had managed to pare the track listing for the two-CD set down to fifty-one songs. When we couldn't agree on which track should ultimately be excluded, the anthology was released with twenty-six songs on disc 1 and twenty-five songs on disc 2. Despite over 100 newspaper and magazine reviews of *50 Coastin' Classics*, not one single critic made reference to the discrepancy.

Over the next few years, I creat-ed numerous country compilations for K-tel, always including songs from the Leiber & Stoller Music Publishing catalog on each release.

Shortly after meeting Owen Husney—as I did with every new music industry contact I made—I sent him a copy of our six-CD promo-pack. So when K-tel's in-house creative team decided to put together a boxed set called *The Brill Building Sound*, Owen called on me to help out with the track selection.

The Brill Building had once been the home of Leiber and Stoller's offices. Located at 1619 Broadway in Manhattan, it had also been the home to many independent record labels and music publishing com-panies during the 1950s and 1960s. Leiber and Stoller, Doc Pomus and Mort Shuman, Jeff Barry and Ellie Greenwich, Paul Simon, and a host of others created hit songs there. Another building just up the street at 1650 Broadway was where song-writers such as Bobby Darin, Gerry Goffin and Carole King, Neil Se-daka and Howie Greenfield, and Barry Mann and Cynthia Weil were all based. Despite the fact that they

~MAKE USE OF YOUR~ TALENTS AND KNOWLEDGE

Before I began my music business journey, I had no idea that something as mundane as being able to type fast would be so instrumental in leading me to where I am today—but it did.

When I was a kid (back in the days of 45-rpm singles), I didn't know just the hit on the A side. I memorized the songs on both sides of the record, the label name and logo—even the number of minutes and seconds of each song. I was a complete record geek. If I had a buck, I bought a single. If I came up with enough money, I'd buy an album.

As I got older, in addition to the hits on the radio, I began paying at-tention to other genres of music: blues, bluegrass, country, country rock, folk, folk rock, rockabilly, hard rock, heavy metal, acid rock, West Coast jazz, Be-bop, reggae, Southern soul, Northern soul, and everything else my ears and pocketbook could handle. I was—and I remain—immersed in music.

As my music trivia knowledge began to escalate to obscene propor-tions, I frequently wondered if I had filled my brain with useless infor-mation, leaving no space for other knowledge that might be necessary to properly function in life (say math, for instance). When I got into radio, I found an outlet for some of that "use-less information." When I began put-ting together compilation albums and writing liner notes, I discovered having so much music-based information in my head actually paid off—literally.

I'll say it again: no cases are typical. Think about the talents you have. What special knowledge is in your brain? Use that talent and knowledge to help you find your own unique way to pitch songs.

were housed in two different buildings, all of these songwriters are generally referred to as being part of the Brill Building Sound.

Our publishing catalog was filled with songs from the Brill Building era, including not just works by Jerry and Mike, but also Barry and Greenwich, Pomus and Shuman, Bobby Darin, and Phil Spector. (We copublished a number of songs cowritten by Phil. *Copublishing* means exactly what it sounds like: one company owns part of the publishing and another company owns the other part.)

When the track listing was finalized for K-tel's *The Brill Building Sound*, I'd managed to get over a dozen songs from our publishing catalog included in the boxed set. But I didn't stop at K-tel and Rhino. I pursued every label and every avenue I could think of to try to get our songs into as many compilation packages as possible.

Today the compilation album market has dropped off considerably, due not only to the reduction in sales of CDs in general, but also because iTunes sells individual tracks, allowing creative buyers to put together their own compilation packages in the form of "playlists."

But like I said earlier, timing is everything. And to add to the never-ending list of clichés, you have to strike while the iron is hot. During the decade of the 1990s—even though I was busy dealing with plenty of personnel and all of that paperwork—I was still able to keep my finger in the creative pie, placing over 400 songs from our publishing catalog on compilation packages.

CHAPTER TWENTY-EIGHT

Not long after *The Muscle Shoals Sound* was released on Rhino, I went to one of the monthly luncheons held by an organization called the Association of Independent Music Publishers. It was 1993, and I was still trying to get to know as many LA music industry people as I could. At the end of the luncheon, a gentleman came up to me and said, "Randy, I just wanted to let you know how much I've been enjoying the Muscle Shoals CD you put together." While I was thanking him, I was also beginning to panic, because he clearly knew who I was, but I couldn't remember having met him before. Luckily, he bailed me out. "I'm David Rosner," he said. "In addition to thanking you for putting together such a great CD, I also wanted to let you know that Neil is getting ready to record an album of songs from the Brill Building era."

(OK, I'm the first to admit that I live in a world filled with luck and coincidence. I've already told you that by being proactive you can help to make your own luck. Unfortunately, coincidence can't be taught.)

At this point in my conversation with David Rosner, I knew three things: his name, that he dug my *Muscle Shoals Sound* CD, and that there was a guy named Neil who was getting ready to record an album of Brill Building songs. After an awkward silence, I finally just came right out and said it: "Neil who?"

David looked at me as if I was from Mars. "Neil *Diamond*,"

Neil Diamond's 1993 album, *Up On the Roof: Songs from the Brill Building.*

he said. (I would later find out that David and Neil had been business partners for decades.)

Since I'd already dug a pretty deep hole for myself, I decided to dig just a little deeper. I told David we certainly had some songs that would be perfect for Neil's project, but I also asked why he hadn't contacted the major music publishing company that now owned most of the songs usually associated with the Brill Building Sound. He said, "I have, and I'm still waiting for somebody to call me back."

I was astonished. By 1993, Neil Diamond was an absolute superstar. The man had been consistently putting out hit records since the mid-1960s—more than two dozen Top 10 singles over the course of a nearly thirty-year career. As if that weren't impressive enough, he was also considered by many to be one of the greatest live performers of the last few decades. Not surprisingly, the three live albums he'd recorded up to that point had all gone multiplatinum.

But apparently the song pluggers at the one major music publishing company that could've ended up with virtually every song on the album if they'd made any effort at all simply couldn't return a phone call. Probably too busy networking.

David gave me his business card, and I headed back to the office. Now I must confess that at that time I wasn't a huge Neil Diamond fan. But if you're going to be a professional song plugger on any level, you don't always have to absolutely love the artist you're selecting songs for. The important thing is to be able to choose songs that will work for that particular singer.

In those days, even though CDs had become the popular medium for commercial releases, CD burners were still ridiculously expensive, and MP3 files didn't exist yet. So just as had been the case when I'd gone song plugging in Nashville a few years earlier, the cassette tape was still the format that publishers used to pitch individual songs to an artist.

I knew Neil Diamond's singing style, and I had a pretty good idea of his vocal range, so I put together a cassette of a dozen songs I felt could possibly work for him. It was a ridiculously large number to pitch at one time, but—as you already know—I had a lot of songs from the Brill Building era to choose from, so I sent the tape to David Rosner, hoping one or two might make the final cut.

A few months later, I got a call from Teressa Rowell at Neil's office, telling me that Neil wanted to include photos in the CD booklet of all the writers with songs on the album. Then she asked if I could send over a photo of Jerry and Mike, which I took as a very good sign. When she asked if I knew where she could get a photo of Jeff Barry and Ellie Greenwich, I couldn't believe it. Now I knew we had at least two songs on the album—or at least I knew there was a strong *possibility* that we had at least two songs on the album.

In the music business, one of the lessons you learn (usually in the worst possible way) is that no song placement is absolutely guaranteed. I've lost count of the times I've been told a song was going to be used, only to discover that it got replaced at the last second. The three rules I've learned to live by are: the song's not on the album until it's been released, the song's not in the movie until the movie is in the theatres, and the song's definitely not in the commercial until you see it on TV.

But this time, things went my way. When Neil Diamond's *Up On the Roof: Songs from the Brill Building* was released in September of 1993, it included six songs from our publishing company: "Love Potion # 9," "Do Wah Diddy Diddy," "I (Who Have Nothing)," "River Deep, Mountain High," "Spanish Harlem," and "Sweets for My Sweet."

A few weeks later, Teressa called me again, this time to tell me Neil was sending me a gold record. All these years later, I still remember her exact words: "Neil wants you to know this isn't coming from the record label. It's coming from him personally." It was at that very moment that I became a huge Neil Diamond fan.

Up On the Roof: Songs from the Brill Building having gone gold, I thought that was the last I'd hear from Neil's camp. After all, he usually wrote most of the songs that appeared on his records, and I wasn't expecting a *Back Up On the Roof:*

~SOCIALIZE—AND NOT JUST OVER THE INTERNET~

There are songwriter organizations in cities all over the country. In and around the three major music spots in the US (Los Angeles, New York, and Nashville), there are not only organizations for songwriters, but also for music publishers and other music-related professionals.

It's fine to socialize via computer or smart phone or whatever other piece of technology you're carrying around, but to be a song plugger you've got to get out there and meet other actual human beings—not just their hand-held devices.

Comedian/TV show host Bill Maher is known for his "New Rules." Here's my New Rule: you can't say you've met somebody if you've never shaken that person's hand.

If you go to the listening session of a songwriter organization some night, it's entirely possible you'll have to sit through some of the worst songs you've ever heard in your life. Believe me, I know. I've been the "guest listener" more times than my ears care to admit. But the point is, I was there. And other people who might turn out to be very important to your career are also frequently called upon to critique songs at listening sessions.

My chance meeting with David Rosner at an Association of Independent Music Publishers luncheon resulted in numerous cuts on two gold records. I didn't go to that luncheon for the gourmet food. I also didn't go there to listen to a bunch of nice people on a dais tell me stuff I already knew. I went there to socialize with my colleagues in the music publishing business.

Every now and then, close your laptop and venture forth among the rest of us. Socialize! Every chance you have to meet someone who matters is another potential chance to pitch your songs.

Songs from the Brill Building, Part 2. But, to my pleasant surprise, two years later he released a two-CD concert album—*Live in America*—that included both "I (Who Have Nothing)" and "River Deep, Mountain High." And as if that weren't a pleasant enough surprise, *Live in America* went gold too.

When the dust finally settled, I'd ended up with eight songs over the course of two albums, both of which had gone gold. As song plugging goes, it wasn't a bad afternoon's work—and I never even had to leave my office.

But the day was slowly approaching when I'd have to do more than leave the office to pitch a tune. When it came to playing the Sinatra Song for Willie Nelson, I'd have to leave the country.

CHAPTER TWENTY-NINE

My pal Roger Deitz had definitely one-upped me by getting to spend some time on the bus with Willie. After all, when it comes to country music shrines, Willie's bus is probably second only to the Ryman Auditorium—original home of the Grand Ole Opry. But anybody can go to Nashville and take the Ryman Auditorium tour. To actually set foot inside of Willie's bus, you have to be invited—either that, or you have to be hanging out with someone else when *they* get invited on board. For my first visit on Willie's bus, I went with option number 2.

As the fates would have it (are you beginning to sense a pattern here?), an old friend of mine from Nashville was compiling a book of conversations with legendary country songwriters. Even though he lived in the very town that 99 percent of all country songwriters call home, he'd flown out to California to interview the handful of country songwriters living on the West Coast. Since Willie was going to be playing a gig at the Cerritos Center for the Performing Arts while my friend was in the area, the amiable author was able to coerce Willie's PR person into providing him with two tickets to the afternoon show and two backstage passes.

In November of 1999, my author friend called to ask if I wanted to go to the concert with him—and, more to the point, asked if I could give him a ride. I hadn't seen Willie since the Roger Miller incident some sixteen years earlier, and I hadn't seen my Nashville friend in a few years either, so I was happy to have the chance to be his chauffeur and go to a Willie Nelson concert for free. I picked him up at his hotel in LA, and we passed the time catching up on each others' lives during the hour-long drive to Cerritos.

I dropped my friend off in front of the "will call" booth so he could wait in line for the tickets and the backstage passes while I found a place to park. The closest spot turned out to be a few feet from Willie's bus. I had read in Roger Deitz's *Acoustic Guitar* article that Willie's bus was called the Honeysuckle Rose II. I walked over to the bus and was admiring the artwork painted on its side when the door suddenly opened and out popped Connie Nelson—also known as Willie's Former Wife III. Connie took one look at me and said, "Hey, I know you! You're the guy from the Songwriters Hall of Fame."

More than sixteen years had passed since I had escorted Willie and Connie into the reception area at the Hall of Fame awards show, but somehow—all those years later, on the opposite coast, totally out of context, and with me in jeans and a T-shirt instead of a rented tuxedo—Connie had recognized me instantly. She leaned close to me and mock-whispered, "Are you surprised to see me? Even though we split up several years ago, Will and I are still friends. I always come to see him when I get the chance."

As Connie walked away, Willie's famous quote about marriage popped into my head: "There is no such thing as ex-wives," he once said. "There are only additional wives."

After the concert was over, I discovered that my author friend wasn't the only one the PR person had doled out backstage passes to. There were dozens of us packed like subway passengers at rush hour in a hallway leading to the back exit of the Cerritos Center. Eventually a security guard opened the exit door; told us to form a line, single file; and pointed us toward the bus—the very bus I had parked right next to, the very bus that none of us needed backstage passes to get to in the first place. There stood Willie by the door of the Honeysuckle Rose II, pen in hand, ready to sign all the flotsam and jetsam the crowd in front of us held before him.

Since my friend was scheduled to do an interview with Nelson, we decided to hang in the back of the line. As an hour or so passed, we waited not-so-patiently in the Cerritos sun, discussing whether or not it was really necessary for every person assembled to tell Willie his or her life story. The most amazing thing, though, was that Willie was willing to stand there and listen to each and every one of them with a Zen-like, blissful smile on his face.

Finally, the last of the here's-my-life storytellers finished her tale. My friend stepped up, said hello to Willie, and told him about the interview he had booked through the PR person. Willie listened patiently and then looked at me. Unlike Connie, Willie's face held no instant recognition—nor should it have. He'd spent the last hour talking to more people than I had spoken to in the last month. As far as Willie knew, I was the very last guy in line—still desperately waiting to tell him my life story.

When my friend introduced me as the guy who came with him to the concert, Willie smiled, said hello, and invited us both onto the bus. As we stepped inside, I saw a gentleman who was—at that time—a guitar player in Willie's band. The guitarist was sitting on the sofa that ran along the wall next to the door. On the sofa facing us sat Willie's sister/piano player, Bobbie Nelson. Willie and my friend headed to that same table in the kitchen area where Roger and Willie had once passed the Jack Daniel's bottle.

I sat on the sofa next to the guitarist who turned to me and—out of the blue—started talking about Chet Baker, the West Coast jazz trumpeter who had been killed in a fall from his hotel room in Amsterdam a little over a decade earlier. When he asked if I knew who Baker was, I told him I had over fifty Chet Baker CDs in my collection, and that Chet had been a friend of both of my bosses. The guitarist's eyes lit up, and then he told me he had played a number of gigs with Chet and that a couple of the shows had been recorded but hadn't yet been released. Since there had been dozens of CDs of Chet's live recordings released by 1999, I made a lame joke about the two live recordings the guitarist did with Chet probably being the only ones still in the can. At that point, the conversation dragged to a halt.

I nervously looked down the hallway of the bus toward Willie and my friend, wondering if I was going to be stuck sitting there for an hour or two while the interview was going on. I'd had high hopes of sitting next to my friend, listening to Willie tell songwriting stories. Instead I was sitting on a sofa, out of earshot of whatever the two of them were discussing at the table just a few feet away.

Since I couldn't hear what they were saying, and since (thanks to my rapier wit and profound stupidity) my conversation with the guitarist was clearly over, I turned to Willie's sister—Bobbie Nelson—the only other person left on the bus.

"Bobbie, I know you don't remember me," I started, "but we actually met in New York in 1983." She smiled sweetly and was kind enough not to say, "You're right. I've got no clue who you are or why you're on this bus."

Even though my friend was the one there to do an interview, the part-time writer in me couldn't help but ask a question I'd pondered for some time: "You're such a great musician, Bobbie. I've always wondered why you haven't recorded a solo album yet."

Just as Bobbie started telling me that she had recently been thinking about that very thing, I realized my friend and Willie were walking toward me. My friend gave me the head nod—the vigorous kind that means "It's time to leave— right now!" I stood up, shook hands with Willie, Bobbie, and Willie's guitarist, thanked Willie for inviting us onto the bus, and headed back into the oppressive Cerritos heat.

"That was a mighty short interview," I said as we got into my car.

My friend looked very dejected. "He told me he didn't realize how long an interview I wanted to do and that we'll need to reschedule it for another time because he's got family in town and they're all getting ready to go out to dinner."

"Bummer. Well, at least now you can tell your kids that you met Willie Nelson and even spent some time with him on his bus. Plus, you got to go to the concert for free."

"Actually," he said, "I had to pay for the round-trip flight and the hotel room in LA, so that was, without question, the most expensive concert I've ever been to."

"Did he at least offer you a swig of Jack Daniel's?" I asked.

"Jack Daniel's? Hell, no!" he said. "I didn't see any booze, but the whole time I was back there, I was staring at the biggest joint I've ever seen in my life, just lying there between us on the table. I was hoping he'd fire that thing up, because I've heard he's got absolutely primo pot."

"Really?" I asked. "Where'd you hear that?"

"In Nashville. Everybody who's ever had Willie share a joint with them says it's really powerful stuff. I've talked to guys who said they couldn't even stand up after a couple of hits. They say the stuff is downright hallucinogenic. One guy told me it's got dried psilocybin mushrooms in it."

"Couldn't even stand up? Hallucinogenic? I've never smoked anything that

Bobbie Nelson's first solo album—*Audiobiography*—was finally released in 2007 (and it was worth the wait).

intense. Well, you missed your chance, I guess."

"You and me both," he said.

"Oh no, not me," I said. "I wouldn't take it if he offered it to me. Who'd want to smoke anything that potent? Quality weed is fine with me, but I don't do mushrooms anymore. No way. Can you imagine sitting on that sofa on Willie's bus, taking a couple of hits off one of his joints, and then realizing you can't stand up—or worse, that you've started tripping? How embarrassing would that be?"

How embarrassing, indeed.

CHAPTER THIRTY

★ ✯ ★

When they were both only nineteen years old, Leiber and Stoller wrote "Kansas City," now one of the best-known blues songs of all time. Little Willie Littlefield, a West Coast–based blues singer, originally recorded the song in 1952. Littlefield's record made some noise regionally but wasn't a hit (one reason probably being due to the record company's last-second decision to change the title from "Kansas City" to "K.C. Loving").

Best Of KANSAS CITY

Great Versions Of Leiber & Stoller's Classic Rock Song

Wilbert Harrison
Lou Rawls
Bill Haley And His Comets
The Everly Brothers

And more great artists sing Kansas City!

K-tel's *Best of "Kansas City"*— Choosing ten great recordings of "Kansas City" was a breeze. Sequencing them in a way that would keep folks from going nuts listening to the same song ten times in a row was a little more difficult.

~EVERYTHING'S RELATIVE

The laws of nature require that everybody be related to somebody—and every once in a while, one of those bodies might be related to somebody who you want to have hear one of your songs.

If you find yourself in the presence of a major act's aunt, uncle, cousin, nephew, or other close relative, I would advise that you proceed with caution. The vast majority of the time—although no doubt wonderful people—Aunt Clara and her kinfolk will probably turn out to be totally useless to you. After all, you really don't need a nineteen-year-old kid who's best known for the ink on his shaved bean to be given a CD of your song by his granddad. I could be wrong, but I'm guessing your chances would be pretty slim of getting Tattoo-Head to cut your tune just because Grandpa Beauregard likes it.

However, I've heard plenty of stories about artists being pitched songs through their relatives. For instance, Billy Edd Wheeler, who cowrote "Jackson" with Jerry Leiber, once told me how the song ended up being recorded by Johnny Cash and June Carter. "Anita Carter's second husband, Don Davis, heard it on one of my Kapp Records albums and took it to Johnny Cash, suggesting it might be a nice duet for him and June." June Carter, being Anita's sister, was Don Davis's sister-in-law.

That single song-pitch by Don the brother-in-law resulted in a Grammy-award-winning country hit for Johnny and June, as well as a major pop hit for Nancy Sinatra and Lee Hazlewood (who cut the song after hearing Johnny and June's version). Thanks to that initial pitch by Don Davis, "Jackson" ended up being recorded by dozens of other duet partners, and was featured twice in the Johnny Cash biopic, *Walk the Line*. Willie Nelson and Sheryl Crow also performed the song together on two separate television appearances.

If you know a relative of someone you feel one of your songs is right for, proceed gently. If you can sense that they're not comfortable with the idea of pitching a song on your behalf, ask them to recommend the proper party you should contact. That way, you take the pressure off the relative and find out vital information at the same time. If your song ends up winning an award and you have to make an acceptance speech on some big TV show, be sure to include that person in the list of folks you're thanking. After all, everything's relative.

Seven years later, Wilbert Harrison recorded the song using the correct title and an arrangement very similar to Littlefield's. Even though it was a blues song, Wilbert's recording flew to No. 1 on the pop charts.

In the ensuing decades, "Kansas City" has become a true standard, performed by numerous blues acts such as Muddy Waters, Albert King, B. B. King, and T-Bone Walker, as well as more mainstream artists—all the way from Little Richard to James Brown to the Beatles to Prince. Since Little Willie Littlefield's record in 1952, there have been literally hundreds of recordings of "Kansas City." It is, without question, the most recorded of all the songs ever written by Leiber and

Stoller. In fact, I once convinced K-tel to put out a CD called *The Best of Kansas City*—a compilation consisting of ten different recordings of the same song!

In the early weeks of the new millennium, I read in *Billboard* that Willie Nelson had decided to cut an all-blues album. Needless to say, I jumped into action. Somehow I managed to acquire the email address of Willie's daughter, Lana Nelson. I sent her a short note, telling her I worked for the guys who wrote "Kansas City" and asking if she knew whether or not her dad had thought about including the song on his blues record. To my pleasant surprise, she actually emailed me back a few days later, saying that she'd talked to him about "Kansas City" and that he'd said he would cut it the following week.

Radio sampler CD of four songs from Willie Nelson's *Milk Cow Blues*, including the Leiber & Stoller classic, "Kansas City."

I probably had nothing to do with Willie's decision to record the song. After all, if you're going to make an album of classic blues tunes, odds are you're going to include "Kansas City." I showed Jerry and Mike the email from Willie's daughter, and all three of us were happy when the song actually appeared—as a duet with Susan Tedeschi—on Nelson's album *Milk Cow Blues*. (Like I said earlier, the song's not on the album until the album's been released.)

CHAPTER THIRTY-ONE

Less than two weeks after *Milk Cow Blues* was released on Island Records, Willie performed at Ray Charles's seventieth birthday celebration at the House of Blues in West Hollywood.

A Memphis-based organization called the Blues Foundation was throwing the party, and an impressive gathering of entertainers was there to perform in Ray's honor. Before the show, Mike Stoller and I went upstairs to the House of Blues Foundation Room for some liquid refreshment, and then across the hall to the Green Room (once again, not green) to pay our respects to Ray. Quincy Jones, Billy Preston, Willie Nelson, Willie's manager, and of course, Ray Charles were all there, smiling at the camera as photographer Lester Cohen snapped away.

When all of the group photos had been taken, I asked Willie if I could get a photo of just the two of us. He smiled that blissful smile and said, "Sure!" As Lester's camera began to flash, Willie asked me what I did for a living. I told him that I worked for Leiber and Stoller—the guys who wrote "Kansas City." I thanked him for recording the song, and then—just like all of those life-storytellers in that long line after the concert in Cerritos—I couldn't stop talking. I said, "Willie, there's no way you're gonna remember this, but you and I first met in 1983 when I was working at the Songwriters Hall of Fame." As Lester began to shoot photos of Willie and me, I continued my story. "I have a picture, framed and hanging on my office wall, of the two of us from that night. In that photo, I have a beautiful head of thick red hair. Seventeen years later, you look exactly the same. I, on the other hand, am now practically bald."

Somewhere in a file drawer at the Blues Foundation in Memphis, Tennessee, there's a contact sheet. On it is a little row of photos of Willie Nelson and yours truly. In one of them, Willie is in the midst of asking me what I do for a living. In the next one, my mouth is wide open as I'm answering his question. In the third shot, Willie's bent over laughing at my hair-loss story.

★ ★ ★ ★ ★

Eventually we all shuffled down to the main floor to watch various artists sing songs mostly made famous by Ray. Willie, naturally, did "Georgia On My Mind," followed by a few of his own. While Nelson was singing "Crazy," the classic hit he wrote for Patsy Cline, I looked across the table and saw Mike staring at someone who was obviously standing right behind me. Mike's eyes were as big as saucers. Jerry's usually the emotional one. Mike is usually less flappable than Mr. Spock. I cautiously looked over my left shoulder. Standing just inches behind my chair was Phil Spector.

Willie and me (and my open mouth) at Ray Charles's seventieth birthday party.

~IT'S NOT ALWAYS A PARTY~

The inevitable moment has come for the obligatory reality check. Being in the music industry is exciting, fun, and a million times better than passing out fliers on the street or working in a poultry plant. But there are some things anyone who's considering a career in the music business should know before attempting to take the plunge. I'm not sharing these things with you now to make you reconsider a possible lifelong career. I'm filling you in so you won't send me an email someday saying, "Why didn't you warn me there was a downside?"

First of all, if you're on the outside, no matter how sexy and glamorous it might look from where you're sitting, be forewarned that there's more paperwork than anybody on the inside would ever want to admit. That paperwork frequently involves math. Luckily, unlike when I was in high school, you get to use a calculator. Other than that, it's still math without all the fun of high school. That's why they call it the music *business* instead of the music *party*. In the decade of the 1970s, there really *was* an ongoing party throughout much of the music industry. The few major record labels in existence today are still paying the tab for that big party in the '70s.

But what about getting to hang out in clubs late into the night, or the free tickets to concerts by major acts, or the star-studded industry events? I'd be the first to admit that they're all great. The only thing you have to remember is that you're going to all of those clubs and concerts and black-tie dinners at night—after you've been at work all day.

And then there are the company mergers and acquisitions. I've known lots of folks who loved the paperwork, the math, the clubbing, the free concerts, and the black-tie events. They didn't mind a bit that their workdays started at ten in the morning and ended at two o'clock the next morning five days a week—not to mention the occasional weekends at the office. Fourteen-hour days require a lot of dedication. Unfortunately, thanks to those mergers and acquisitions, all that dedication frequently turns out to be rewarded with a pink slip, thanks to that big company those folks work for getting purchased by an even bigger company.

Consider this: There used to be a major publishing company called Warner Bros. Music and another major publishing company called Chappell & Co. Now there's Warner/Chappell Music. There used to be a major publishing company called MCA Music and another major publishing company called PolyGram. Jointly they became Universal Music Publishing. Sony Music acquired Tree Music and became Sony Tree. Michael Jackson bought a company called ATV. Among other things, it included a company called Northern Songs that consisted of the Beatles' publishing catalog. Sony, Tree, and ATV are now all one big company called Sony/ATV Music. There used to be a major publishing company called BMG Music, which is now owned by the aforementioned Universal Music. I could waste pages giving more examples.

By the way, if you're a songwriter thinking none of the above affects you, what if you were signed to one of those publishing companies that got swallowed up by another? The size of that mammoth company's catalog would be greatly increased, while the importance of your songs would be diminished due to the sheer volume of copyrights all being under the same roof.

But despite the host of mergers and acquisitions that have taken place in the music publishing business, they don't hold a candle to the consolidation among record labels.

The point is this: every time a publishing company or a record label gets bought, there is suddenly an excess of personnel. In business, nothing is less tolerable than excess personnel.

I've always felt that the British have the best phrase for being let go. In England, the recently unemployed don't say they've been canned or fired or laid off. They say they've been "made redundant." In the world of music business mergers and acquisitions, that's usually literally the case. If the purchasing company has a royalty department head and the company being purchased has a royalty department head, one of those heads is going to roll.

If you're a songwriter who's developed a great relationship with the creative personnel at the publishing company you're signed to, what's going to happen to you when every last person you've been working with is let go in one fell swoop?

If you're a song plugger with close ties to the A&R folks at a label that's just been bought, those A&R execs aren't going to be able to do you much good when they're out on the street looking for jobs.

To paraphrase a Kris Kristofferson song, you have to decide if you think the good times will outweigh the bad. Personally, I've lived through it all by gingerly leaping over the landmines, so far, my entire career. And despite the downsides, I can honestly say the good times have stomped all over the bad times. And even though I know it's not always a party, I know there's going to be another one coming soon. Just gotta take care of a little paperwork first.

Jerry, Mike, and Phil went back a long way—too long, in fact. Although Jerry and Phil had written "Spanish Harlem" together in 1961—a massive hit for both Ben E. King and Aretha Franklin—the relationship between the three men had soured over the years. As surreal as it was to watch Jerry and Mike each obligingly hugging Phil that night, things would become even more surreal less than three years later, when actress Lana Clarkson—hostess of the very same House of Blues Foundation Room Mike and I had been in earlier that evening—would be found dead from a pistol shot to the head in Spector's house in Alhambra.

★ ★ ★ ★ ★

A few weeks after Ray Charles's party, I received an 8" x 10" glossy photo in the mail. Despite the fact that some genius at the Blues Foundation had decided the best of the three photos from that contact sheet was the one of me with my mouth wide open, I framed it anyway and hung it on my Wall of Fame, along with the autographed photo of Willie and the other photo of Willie and me from 1983—the one from the days when I still had that beautiful head of thick red hair.

CHAPTER THIRTY-TWO

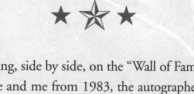

So there they hung, side by side, on the "Wall of Fame" in my office: the photo of Willie and me from 1983, the autographed photo from Willie dated 1993, and the open-mouthed photo of me with Willie from October of 2000. The remaining photographs on the wall of yours truly posing with all of those other celebrities could have been—and in fact, for the most part were—pictures quickly snapped at various industry functions over the course of my decades in the music business. But the three Willie photos hanging there together tended to give the impression to even the most casual observer that he and I were more than just passing acquaintances. Hey, if people wanted to think that was really the case, it was fine with me.

I'm sure there are people out there who aren't fans of Willie's music or his acting or his politics or his pot smoking, but nobody ever walked into my office, saw those three photos, and then said to me, "I don't like Willie Nelson." To the contrary, everyone who ever commented on the photos of Willie—from suit-and-tied executives to nose-pierced interns—had the same animated reaction: "You *know* Willie Nelson???"

Willie Nelson's life story has been told in book form by, among others, Nelson himself (*Willie: An Autobiography*); Joe Nick Patoski (*Willie Nelson: An Epic Life*); Graeme Thomson (*Willie Nelson: The Outlaw*); Michael Bane (*Willie: An Unauthorized Biography of Willie Nelson*); his daughter Susie (*Heart Worn Memories: A Daughter's Personal Biography of Willie Nelson*); and his daughter Lana (*Willie Nelson Family Album*). He was even portrayed as a fictional version of himself in Kinky Friedman's mystery novel *Road Kill*. Willie Nelson's story has been told so many times that there's little need for

Willie Nelson: An Epic Life by noted Texas author, Joe Nick Patoski.

AN EPIC LIFE

WILLIE NELSON

JOE NICK PATOSKI

me to go into great detail about his background here. But just in case you're not familiar with how Willie became an American icon, here is the condensed version of all of the above (except the mystery novel):

Willie was born in Abbott, Texas, in April of 1933. His sister, Bobbie, was born two years earlier. Willie and Bobbie's parents split up only weeks after Willie's birth. When Willie was six months old, his mother, Myrle, moved to Oklahoma. His father, Ira, remained in Abbott for a while, but turned over the raising of both Willie and Bobbie to his parents, Alfred and Nancy Nelson.

Nancy began giving piano lessons to Bobbie, whom she immediately discovered to be a natural musician. When Willie was six years old, his grandparents gave him a Stella guitar. Alfred showed Willie how to play a few chords, and by the following year, seven-year-old Willie Nelson had begun writing songs.

When Alfred brought home a Philco radio, Willie and Bobbie were exposed to music far beyond what they had been listening to at Abbott Methodist Church. Inspired by the different genres of music they heard over the airwaves, Willie developed his own unique style of guitar playing, while Bobbie greatly expanded her piano repertoire.

Before he was ten years old, Willie was already performing live with local bands. In 1947, while still in high school, he joined Bobbie's husband's band—Bud Fletcher and the Texans—as vocalist and lead guitarist. Bobbie, of course, was the group's pianist.

Willie graduated from high school in 1950 and joined the air force shortly thereafter. Nine months later, he was discharged due to back problems. In 1952, he married his first wife, Martha Matthews.

Although he made money playing and singing in various bands, it wasn't enough for a married man to live on—especially once Lana, the first of his children, was born in 1953. Willie took jobs selling Bibles, encyclopedias, vacuum cleaners, and sewing machines, but music was his passion.

Over the next few years, he became a disc jockey at several radio stations in Texas and Washington, still writing songs and performing live when gigs were available.

Seemingly always on the move, Nelson ended up in Houston in the late 1950s with an impressive catalog of original songs, including one called "Family Bible." In need of money, he sold all rights to the song to a Houston guitar instructor for $50. Shortly thereafter, Claude Gray recorded "Family Bible," and Willie watched as the song he sold for $50 rode its way to the Top 10 on the country charts. To Willie that meant just one thing: it was now clear he could write a country hit, so it was time to move to Nashville.

Arriving in Music City in 1960, Willie began spending his evenings at Tootsie's Orchid Lounge, a tavern directly across the alley from the Ryman Auditorium—at that time, the home of the Grand Ole Opry. It was an inspired move by the aspiring songwriter. Tootsie's was the watering hole for many of the acts performing at the Opry. It was also the hangout for songwriters such as Roger Miller, Hank Cochran, and Harlan Howard.

When Willie sang some of the songs he'd written to a small gathering at Tootsie's one night, Hank Cochran was so excited by what he'd heard that he went to his own publisher, Pamper Music, and convinced the owners to sign Willie to a contract as well. Over the next three years, Willie wrote hits for Patsy Cline ("Crazy"), Ray Price ("Night Life"), Billy Walker ("Hello Walls"), and Faron Young ("Funny How Time Slips Away").

Even though it was rewarding to have others record his songs, Willie Nelson was determined to become a successful recording artist himself. In the midst of his flurry of early country hits as a songwriter, Willie was signed to Liberty Records. In 1962, he had a Top 10 country hit called "Willingly"—a duet with Shirley Collie (who would become his second wife in 1963) and then a second Top 10 country single as a solo artist with "Touch Me." At that point, it looked as if he was going to explode onto the country music scene. But his next single, "Half a Man," turned out to be half a hit. After one more low-charting single for Liberty, the label closed its country division.

It appeared that Willie was taking a major step up when he moved over to RCA Records in 1965. Over the next seven years, Chet Atkins and other top Nashville producers tried their hands at turning Willie into a country star. They all failed.

After more than a dozen albums and singles released by RCA, if the general public knew Willie's name at all, it wasn't because he'd had any major hits on the label but because fellow Texan Don Meredith made occasional references to the singer on ABC TV's *Monday Night Football*. (Clearly a Willie fan, when the outcome of a game was obvious, Meredith would always sing a few lines of Nelson's song, "The Party's Over.")

Around the same time Atlantic Records decided to open a Nashville office in the early 1970s, Willie's days at RCA were mercifully coming to an end. In fact, his days of living in Nashville had also pretty much come to an end, thanks to his house there burning down in December of 1970.

Moving from Nashville, Tennessee, to Austin, Texas, brought about major changes for Willie Nelson. He grew a beard, let his hair grow well past respectable country star standards, and discovered that the music fans in Austin—no matter what their age, occupation, or political affiliation—were open to the music he was making.

The move to Texas also brought out Willie's entrepreneurial side. In 1973, he put on the first in a series of annual music festivals in his home state. The acts he booked for the inaugural event included Waylon Jennings, Kris Kristofferson, Rita

Coolidge, Leon Russell, and Loretta Lynn—all major stars of the day. In a stroke of brilliance (if not a little hubris), he called it "Willie Nelson's Fourth of July Picnic." Thousands attended the festival because of Waylon, Kris, and the other well-known names on the bill—and if they'd never heard of Willie Nelson before, they would now. With his name in the title of the show, he was at the top of the bill.

Once word got out that Willie and RCA had parted ways, Atlantic Records went after Nelson. The singer signed with the label and released two critically acclaimed albums for the label: *Shotgun Willie* in 1973 and *Phases and Stages* in 1974. Reminiscent of his days on Liberty Records, Willie had a duet hit called "After the Fire Is Gone" with fellow Atlantic act Tracy Nelson (no relation), as well as a Top 20 solo hit with "Bloody Mary Morning." And just when it looked like his time had finally come, Atlantic Records bowed out of the country music business.

Luckily, Columbia Records was willing to take a chance on Nelson. After so many years of working with various (otherwise) successful RCA record producers who, in Willie's case, couldn't create a single track of interest to the record-buying public, the singer agreed to sign with Columbia as long as he could control his own destiny. Today it seems almost laughable. In a recording career that had spanned thirteen years by 1975, Willie Nelson's last (and only) Top 10 hit as a solo artist had been back in 1962! The fact that any label wanted to sign him was significant enough. That Columbia would agree to give Willie total creative control is damn near unbelievable. But that's exactly what happened.

★ ★ ★ ★ ★

Willie had been singing the Carl Stutz/Edith L. Calisch song "Red Headed Stranger" for years. Originally popularized by Arthur Smith and His Crackerjacks, Nelson played Smith's recording during his days as a deejay. He also sang it to his children as he was putting them to bed at night. In need of songs for his first album on Columbia, Willie decided "Red Headed Stranger" would be his starting point.

Driving back to Texas from a Colorado ski trip, he told his wife Connie that he needed to come up with more songs for the album. As he drove, she wrote down his song ideas—songs written by others that he wanted to include on the record, as well as lyrics for original songs that he came up with during the long drive home.

A few days later, Willie went into Autumn Sound in Garland, Texas, with his band: Bobbie Nelson (piano), Jody Payne (guitar), Mickey Raphael (harmonica), Bucky Meadows (piano on some tracks, guitar on others), Bee Spears (bass), Paul English (drums), and Billy English (percussion).

It took less than two days to record the entire *Red Headed Stranger* album. Consisting of fifteen songs, the finished recording was sparse, dark, and totally original. No one had ever made a record like it—country or otherwise. A combination of new songs by Willie and country standards such as "Blue Eyes Crying in the Rain," *Red Headed Stranger* was a concept album set in the Old West at the turn of the twentieth century, telling the story of a minister who kills his wife after finding her with another man. As the story unfolds through the songs, the listener hears an unsettling tale of sin and redemption.

This was the mid-1970s—an era when country's airwaves were ruled by Billy "Crash" Craddock, Ronnie Milsap, Mickey Gilley, T. G. Sheppard, Conway Twitty, B. J. Thomas, Tanya Tucker, John Denver, and Glen Campbell. Granted, they were all major talents in their own way, but they were artists whose records were generally filled with strings and backing vocals, and their songs were about lovin', cheatin', truck drivin', and rhinestone cowboys.

When the executives at Columbia Records first heard the album Willie Nelson had submitted for release, they were stunned—and not in a good way. Both the head of the label and the head of Columbia's Nashville division felt it had no commercial potential whatsoever. But Willie had complete artistic control of his recordings, so the album was released, along with the single, "Blue Eyes Crying in the Rain."

Written by Fred Rose, and originally recorded by Roy Acuff in 1945, Willie's version of "Blue Eyes Crying in the Rain" consisted of two acoustic guitars, a bass guitar, and a harmonica, with Willie on lead vocal. Near the end of the song, Willie overdubbed a harmony vocal part over a single line of the song. And that was it. No strings, no background choir, no fiddles, no steel—not even drums. The instrumental cupboard was practically bare. And to the surprise of everyone who was supposed to be "in the know" about such things, "Blue Eyes Crying in the Rain" rocketed to the top of the country charts. It even went to No. 21 on the pop charts!

Red Headed Stranger also went to No. 1 on the country album charts and reached the Top 30 on the pop album charts. For the first time in his thirteen-year

~ THE WILLIE WAY ~

Willie Nelson's very last official album release as a solo artist on RCA Records was titled, ironically, *The Willie Way*. During his seven years of being signed to the label, Willie had almost never gotten his way. It wasn't until he escaped the trappings and regulations of Nashville record making that he finally achieved his greatest success.

For most people, playing by the rules is the safe and proper way to go through life. (Here's hoping the accountant who does my taxes and all of my doctors fall into this category.) For the exclusive few—the one-of-a-kinds—success comes only after the rulebook has been tossed aside.

When Willie Nelson arrived in Nashville with his catalog of songs, the general complaint was that they weren't country enough. He was told his songs had too many chords to be country. His style of guitar playing also seemed too esoteric for most people to appreciate. A lot of folks didn't like his singing voice or his unique vocal phrasing. But he wasn't deterred by the opinions of others, and he didn't give up just because he wasn't able to put together a string of hits as a recording artist.

He didn't give up after three albums, or six, or nine, or twelve, or fifteen. Can you imagine? As the years passed, he just kept making records, writing songs, and playing gigs. Clearly, he was absolutely determined to make it.

Everything appeared to finally be going his way when his two Atlantic releases (albums number 16 and 17) garnered more press and rave reviews than the previous fifteen combined. But when Atlantic announced that it was closing its country division, he still didn't give up.

Red Headed Stranger was Willie Nelson's eighteenth album—the album that not only turned him into a star but also proved that he had been right all along. To finally achieve success on a grand scale, he simply needed to do things the Willie Way.

When it comes to song plugging, determination is a requisite. And if you are to be successful, you'll need to follow Winston Churchill's advice. "Never give in. Never, never, never, never." If Willie Nelson had given in and called it quits after his seventeenth album, no one would have blamed him—and most of us would have never heard of him. But he didn't give up, and today his music, his acting, and his activism are known throughout the world.

To be a successful song plugger, you have to be determined to keep plugging away, no matter how much rejection you might face. Although getting a specific song recorded by a specific artist is the ultimate goal, there's never any guarantee that it will actually happen. In fact, the greatest song pluggers in the world still have extremely low batting averages.

The failure rate in song plugging reminds me of a story my dad once told me about a rather homely young man named Doug. He told me Doug would say hello to every female he saw. It didn't matter where or when. If he was walking down the street, he'd say hello to each woman who passed by. If he was in a room full of people, he said hello to every lady there. If he was on a bus, the subway, or an airplane, no woman would escape his greeting. After seeing this phenomenon in person on numerous occasions, my dad finally asked Doug why he had this compulsion to say hello to every last woman he encountered. Doug told him, "I've looked in the mirror, so I know my only option is to go with the law of averages. I say hello to all women because I know sooner or later, one of them is going to say hello back to me."

The theory behind song plugging is very similar to Doug's theory on meeting women. If you believe in the song, you might need to be a tad more selective than Doug was, but even though you might get turned down time and again, it doesn't mean that "they" are all correct and that you're the one who's wrong. If you don't believe me, just ask Willie.

recording career, Willie Nelson had finally made an album his way. And lo and behold—after all those years of being forced make records the way other people wanted him to—it turned out that all the experts were wrong and the first-time record producer was right. After *Red Headed Stranger*, there was no looking back.

Over the next decade, seven more Willie Nelson albums would reach the top of the country charts. During that same time span, Willie scored seventeen more No. 1

singles, including "Always On My Mind," which also made it to No. 5 on the pop charts. The *Stardust* album alone spawned three hit singles. And then the movies began.

Willie appeared first in the Robert Redford/Jane Fonda film *Electric Horseman*—with a soundtrack that included the No. 1 hit "My Heroes Have Always Been Cowboys." His first starring role was in *Honeysuckle Rose*, a movie that included two more No. 1 hits: "Angel Flying Too Close to the Ground," and the song that has become the theme of Willie's life, "On the Road Again."

And of course there were the duet hits—with Waylon Jennings, Ray Charles, Merle Haggard, Julio Iglesias, his old friends Roger Miller and Ray Price, Leon Russell, Toby Keith, and others. As if that weren't enough, he also had hit singles and albums with his country supergroup, the Highwaymen (Willie, Waylon, Kris Kristofferson, and Johnny Cash).

There have been some serious hiccups along the way—problems with the IRS and more than one arrest on drug charges—but through it all, Willie Nelson has never stopped making music.

He has received Grammy Awards, CMA Awards, ACM Awards, American Music Awards, and others. He's been inducted into the Songwriters Hall of Fame and the Country Music Hall of Fame. He's been a Kennedy Center Honoree and the guest of several presidents. (He even smoked pot on the roof of the White House during the Carter administration.)

Like Bob Dylan (another of his duet partners), Willie Nelson changed the musical landscape. The term "outlaw country" was created for the kind of music he and pals such as Waylon Jennings began to make in the 1970s.

Willie unsuccessfully tried to play the Nashville game for over a decade before he finally realized that the only way to beat the system was to break virtually all of the rules Nashville had ever written. A line from his song "Me and Paul," captured all of those misspent years in a single phrase: "Nashville was the roughest."

CHAPTER THIRTY-THREE

★ ✮ ★

It was the fourth of May 2006—*carpe diem* time. As happens to just about everyone who's ever owned a computer, mine had crashed a few months earlier, taking Lana Nelson's email address with it. So even though Willie's daughter had been the one to confirm that Willie was recording "Kansas City" six years earlier, this time she wasn't an option. For the life of me, I couldn't remember how I'd gotten her email address in the first place, and now there wasn't time to try to get it again.

My first move was to dig through one of my Rolodexes* and find Willie's manager's phone number. When the receptionist answered, I told her who I was and asked to speak to Mark. After I'd been kept on hold for an eternity, she came back on the line, asking what the call was regarding. I told her I had a song that Leiber and Stoller wanted Willie to hear. I went back on hold for another eternity before the receptionist came back on again and told me that Mark was on a phone call at the moment and would have to call me back. It didn't take Sherlock Holmes to figure out that she could've told me that the instant I called, so it was "Strike 1" for Randy.

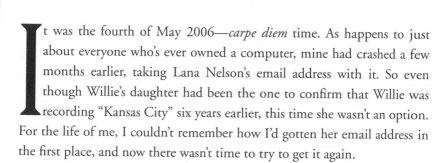

I went back to pollstar.com to see where in Canada Willie was at the moment and tried to figure out where I could catch

. . . .
* Since Rolodexes are almost as obsolete as typewriters, allow me to explain: A Rolodex was a spindle with a giant knob on each end. The spindle held cards on which were typed the names, addresses, and phone numbers of the Rolodex owner's friends, business associates, favorite restaurants, doctors, lawyers, and so forth. In Hollywood—back before everyone started putting all of their contacts on computer databases—often a person's power in the industry was judged by the number of Rolodexes he or she had. "Mary must be really important. When I went walked by her office today, I saw four Rolodexes on her desk."

up with him if I could get the whole trip to come together in the next week or so. He was moving across the country so quickly that I realized by the time I'd have a chance to catch up with him he could be as far away as Newfoundland.

After a bit of research on the Internet, I found out the name of Willie's PR person. I couldn't find an email address, but I found a street address and wrote her a warm and fuzzy letter, telling her about Jerry and Mike and "The Girls I Never Kissed," about how Frank Sinatra had recorded the song back in the 1980s, about needing to set up a meeting with Willie while he was in Canada, and about not being able to get Willie's manager on the phone.

I sent the letter, a Leiber and Stoller press kit, an article about L&S that had

~KEEP TRACK OF YOUR CONTACTS~

If you've been following the bouncing ball, you know by now that your primary objective is to get to know anyone and everyone in the business. Don't just know *of* them—know their names, know their faces, know where they work, know their titles, know their wives' or husbands' names, know their kids' names, know their pets' names, know their hobbies, know their birthdays, know what music they like, know what music they don't like. Get the numbers of their direct lines, get their cell phone numbers, get their email addresses, get the URLs of their websites.

Needless to say, you're not going to find out everything about anyone the first time you meet him or her. It takes a while to cultivate relationships in the music business. Getting to know people over time is one of the main reasons God invented business lunches. And of course, you also have to make sure people know you. The more information you offer up about yourself, the more likely they are to provide information about themselves to you.

Every person you get to know in the entertainment business is a potential portal that could lead to you getting a song recorded or used in a film, TV show, and so forth. Referring to a person as a portal might sound rather impersonal, but in the music business, it really isn't. I'd much rather be able to say I was instrumental in helping   you get one of your songs used in a major motion picture than to be able to say I was the jerk who prevented you from it. After all, if I help you, there's a good chance you'll be happy to help me if I'm in need of a favor someday.

But for anything to be set in motion, the first thing we have to do is know each other. And we have to write that information down, whether it's handwritten on an old-fashioned Rolodex or entered into the latest technological gizmo. Whatever method you use, the important thing is to create your own database of contact information. I promise, it will serve you well.

appeared in the *Los Angeles Times* Sunday magazine section just days earlier, and a CD of the Sinatra Song to her via Federal Express. Then I sat back and waited for nothing to happen.

To my surprise, an email arrived from her the very next day. It was beautifully written and extremely polite. And of course, it said that she couldn't help me because Willie's manager was the only one who could authorize the meeting I was requesting. Without question, it was the nicest rejection I've ever gotten—and being both a music publisher and an author, I've gotten plenty of rejections over the years. The email concluded with the sentence "Please let me know if there is anything else I can do for you."

I was tempted to write her back and say, "Yes, there is something else you can do for me. Please shoot me so I won't have to face Jerry Leiber and admit I don't know how to get this song to Willie." Instead I just wrote, "Not to worry. I'm sure I'll find some other way to get the song to him."

In truth, I wasn't at all sure that I'd find some other way to get the song to him. The only thing I knew for sure was that I'd swung at another one and missed. "Strike 2."

CHAPTER THIRTY-FOUR

Tis strange—but true; for truth is always strange;
Stranger than fiction . . .

—Lord Byron, *Don Juan*, canto 14, stanza 101

It's time for another cliché—and as far as my pitching the Sinatra Song to Willie Nelson is concerned, this next one is pretty damn apropos. Every cliché is the result of someone somewhere in the course of history coming up with a truism so perfectly encapsulated in a single phrase that it catches on with the general public and is ultimately so overused that as a rule, writers avoid them. As you've noticed by now, I'm ignoring that rule. Plus, I figure if it's good enough for Lord Byron, it's certainly good enough for me. Byron's lines from *Don Juan* would eventually be truncated down to simply this: "Truth is stranger than fiction." And so it is.

Despite my full-time day job running Jerry and Mike's music publishing companies, I've always had plenty of free time due to an inability to sleep more than four or five hours a night—a malady I developed when I moved from a sleepy Alabama hamlet to the open-all-night city of New York. So after years of lying in bed, staring at the ceiling from midnight to about four a.m., I decided it would be more productive if I sat at my computer in my home office and wrote during those hours. By 2006, I had pumped out two books, dozens of articles for various music-oriented magazines, and the liner notes to over 100 albums (many of those albums being ones I had compiled for Rhino, K-tel, Warner Bros., and other labels).

In May of 2006, I was putting the finishing touches on the book I was writing about Duane Allman. A couple of years earlier, the very first person I had interviewed for the book was the Nitty Gritty Dirt Band's John McEuen. Bill McEuen—John's brother—was already the Dirt Band's manager when he discovered Duane Allman and his brother, Gregg, playing at a club in St. Louis, Missouri, in the mid-1960s. Bill encouraged the two lads and their fellow band-mates to move to Los Angeles, which they promptly did—soon sharing space in a house that was also home to John McEuen and the rest of the members of the Nitty Gritty Dirt Band.

In short order, Bill McEuen had gotten Duane's band, the Hour Glass, signed to Liberty Records—the same label Bill had earlier gotten the Nitty Gritty Dirt Band signed to (and coincidentally, the same label Willie Nelson had re-corded for at the beginning of his career). A close friendship formed between the members of the two bands. John even played banjo on a couple of songs for the Hour Glass's first album.

I had met John over the Internet in 1989, so when I started writing the Duane Allman book in 2004, I gave him a call. John agreed to let me interview him, and a number of the stories he told me about Allman ended up in the book.

During a break in the interview, John just happened to tell me a story about an experience he'd had in Vegas involving Willie Nelson. Now as I sat at my desk two years after I'd interviewed him, I couldn't remember anything about John's story except that the setting was Vegas and the subject was Willie Nelson. I didn't know how well John knew Willie. All I knew was that he'd told me about a conversation they'd once had in Sin City. But after having no luck with Willie's manager or Willie's PR person, I was reaching the desperation point. I'd gone through all of my Rolodexes and hadn't come up with anyone else I thought might be able to connect me with Willie. John McEuen was my last hope—and my potential "Strike 3."

When I called John's house, I got his answering machine. I hung up the phone without leaving a message. I tried to stay calm, but I knew John could be almost anywhere. He was always playing a gig, sometimes as a solo act and sometimes with the still-together-after-nearly-forty-years Nitty Gritty Dirt Band.

Just as I had done when I was trying to figure out where Willie was, I went

John McEuen

back to pollstar.com and typed "John McEuen" in the little box. There was one date listed for a May 21st solo gig at McCabe's in Santa Monica. It was now May 5th. I couldn't wait until May 21st. I had to get in touch with John *now*. So, I typed in "Nitty Gritty Dirt Band," and a list of dates and cities appeared on my screen. It read, "May 5—Fredericton, New Brunswick; May 6—Moncton, New Brunswick; May 7—Charlottetown, Prince Edward Island; May 9—St. John, Nova Scotia; May 10—Halifax, Nova Scotia; May 11—Sydney, Nova Scotia; May 13—Corner Brook, Newfoundland."

I could feel my heart rate actually starting to increase. Could this really be happening? I typed in Willie's name again and there it was: "May 5—Fredericton, New Brunswick; May 6—Moncton, New Brunswick; May 7—Charlottetown, Prince Edward Island; May 9—St. John, Nova Scotia; May 10—Halifax, Nova Scotia; May 11—Sydney, Nova Scotia; May 13—Corner Brook, Newfoundland."

It seemed absolutely impossible—the ultimate coincidence. The odds were completely off the charts. Truth is, indeed, so much stranger than fiction. The Nitty Gritty Dirt Band was playing on the same bill with Willie Nelson—all the way across Canada.

I grinned from ear to ear, reached into my desk drawer, pulled out the bottle of Gentleman Jack I've always kept on hand for only the most special of occasions—and raised a toast to good ol' Lord Byron.

CHAPTER THIRTY-FIVE

As I said in the first chapter of this book, I've worked at the same company since 1985. I couldn't have stayed at the same job for so long if I didn't love it. My longstanding joke has been that I work for free—I get paid to drive in LA traffic to and from my office five times a week.

Song plugging is only a small part of my job, but I enjoy it because I have such a great catalog of songs to promote. I can't imagine what it would be like to have to pitch songs I didn't believe in.

The main reason I got into the music business is because I love music. My entire life revolves around it, and vice versa. I became obsessed with the music of Bob Dylan, the Beatles, the Rolling Stones, the Who, the Allman Brothers, and many others as an adolescent, and that obsession never really went away. It's probably safe to say that I'm still an adolescent in many ways, much to the chagrin of plenty of people who wish I'd get on with it and grow up. Not a chance.

★ ★ ★ ★ ★

The reason I'd made it a point to get to know John McEuen in the first place was because my music-obsessed adolescence (and so-called adulthood) was more his band's fault than it was Dylan's, the Beatles', the Stones', the Who's, or any of the other acts I was listening to at the time.

In November of 1970, the Nitty Gritty Dirt Band hit the charts with a Jerry Jeff Walker–penned song called "Mr. Bojangles"—a track from the now-classic album *Uncle Charlie & His Dog Teddy*. The following year, my sister called me from her dorm room to tell me that the band was going to be playing at her college. I was fifteen years old, and my sister's school was 100 miles from where I lived, but I knew I had to find a way to see the Nitty Gritty Dirt Band live in concert. I called my sixteen-year-old friend Jon Page and told him to come over to my house as soon as possible. When he got there, I told my mother that Jon and I had to go to Bolivar, Missouri, because we both wanted to see this band, and that Jon had volunteered to drive me there. This was, of course, a blatant fabrication. There was no way Jon's parents were going to let him drive all the way to Bolivar when the ink wasn't even dry on his driver's license yet. So my mother insisted on taking us. The plan had worked.

When we got to the concert, the place was packed, but we managed to get seats in the front row of the balcony. I can still remember everything vividly. The primary lead singer was Jeff Hanna, who also played guitar; Les Thompson

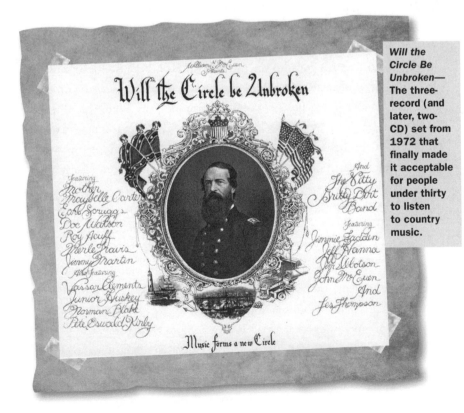

Will the Circle Be Unbroken—The three-record (and later, two-CD) set from 1972 that finally made it acceptable for people under thirty to listen to country music.

played bass; Jimmy Ibbotson, Jimmie Fadden, and Jeff Hanna switched off on drums—Ibbotson playing harmonica or guitar when Ibbotson was drumming. And, when Ibbotson and Fadden were both occupied with other instruments, Jeff Hanna sat down behind the drum kit. Jimmy and Jimmie both sang, too. And then there was John McEuen. I was amazed that this one guy could switch from guitar to mandolin to banjo to accordion—clearly a master of every musical instrument he picked up. But the instrument that sticks out most in my recollection of that life-changing evening was his fiddle. That night, McEuen was wearing a buckskin outfit with fringed sleeves. When he'd take a solo on the fiddle, he'd literally run back and forth across the stage, bow flying back and forth across the strings as the fringe on his jacket flew back and forth like wheat in a windstorm. He was extremely tall, had long brown hair, and a very thick beard. It was almost more than my fifteen-year-old mind could fathom. Until that night, I didn't even know that a human being could play more than one instrument. John McEuen seemed to be able to play *all* of them.

In 1972, the band would release a triple-record set called *Will the Circle Be Unbroken*—a masterwork that introduced traditional country music to a young, primarily rock-oriented audience. The album featured a host of early country stars, including Mother Mabel Carter, Earl Scruggs, Merle Travis, and Roy Acuff (the man who had the first hit version of "Blue Eyes Crying in the Rain" back in 1945). The Nitty Gritty Dirt Band's *Will the Circle Be Unbroken* album preceded Willie Nelson's *Red Headed Stranger* by three years, undoubtedly helping pave the way for Willie to be accepted by an audience that stretched far beyond the bounds of dyed-in-the-wool country music fans. And so it goes.

After moving to Los Angeles in 1989, I happened to meet John McEuen not long after I decided to find out what this new thing called the Internet was all about. I bought a modem, got it hooked up, and started playing around in cyberspace. If you weren't there at the time, you have no idea how primitive it was. It seemed like there were only a handful of us rooting around, trying to figure the thing out. In those earliest days, having an email address was akin to having a private phone number. Well-known celebrities didn't even try to keep their email addresses a secret, because there were only a handful of people around to email them in the first place.

~MUSIC LOVERS UNITE!~

If your primary reason for wanting to be involved with the music industry in any way is to make tons of money, my advice is to pick a different profession—and *pronto*.

If music isn't your life, you shouldn't waste time trying to make it your life's work. There are plenty of other ways to earn respectable amounts of money that aren't nearly as competitive and don't involve anywhere near the amount of rejection songwriters and song pluggers are subjected to. Remember the chewing gum commercial with the tag line "Double your pleasure?" If you're a songwriter pitching your own tunes, you'll frequently have to deal with double the rejection.

In the music business, you absolutely must have a passion for what you're doing. If you don't believe in the songs you're plugging, why should the people you're pitching them to?

Since you're reading this book, I suspect you're one of "us"—music lovers who've chosen to try to make a living by immersing ourselves in a world of lyrics and melodies.

The beauty of song plugging is that you don't have to be a musical virtuoso. Unlike those early pluggers, you don't even have to be able to read music. Passion, on the other hand, is a necessity.

One day I saw a post by John McEuen on some early, primitive forum. And there, at the end of his post, was his email address. I sent him an email, asking if he was the same John McEuen who had been a member of the Nitty Gritty Dirt Band. (John had left the band in 1986, but, luckily for me, would return in 2001.) He wrote back and said that indeed he was. My next email to him was to tell him that I had seen his band—the first concert I'd ever been to—when I was fifteen years old. I told him who I was, who I worked for, and that having gone to that concert in 1971 was the impetus for my choosing the music business as a career path.

John was living in Colorado at the time but would eventually move to LA, after which we began to occasionally get together for lunch when he wasn't on the road. His long brown hair was now a bit shorter and had turned silver, as had his beard. But I could still envision him running across the stage, sawing away on that fiddle.

Now that I had discovered the serendipitous coincidence that the Nitty Gritty Dirt Band was opening for Willie on his Canadian tour,

I knew the best chance of getting in touch with John was the same way I'd met him back in 1989.

I checked the Rolodex card for his email address and began to write:

> Dear John,
> I see that you and the boys are in Canada at the moment, do-ing some gigs with Willie. I've got a Leiber and Stoller song I need to play for Willie, but I can't get his manager on the phone and the PR lady says she can't help me without the manager's stamp of approval. If I fly to Canada sometime next week, can you hook me up with him?
> Best,
> Randy

Of course, I didn't know if John had his laptop with him—or if he even had a laptop. I also had no clue what kind of Internet access he might have in Canada. But less than an hour later I got a reply:

> Randy,
> I can easily introduce you to Willie. I am sure he would listen to the song. It's a good place to do it . . . fewer distractions than LA or a big city gig.
> John

A couple of hours earlier, I had been in a total panic about how I was going to make contact with Willie Nelson. Now it seemed almost too easy.

CHAPTER THIRTY-SIX

★ ✦ ★

On Saturday, May 6th, I sat in front of my laptop, going from one travel site to another, trying to figure out how to get myself from Los Angeles, California, to Sydney, Nova Scotia. Thanks to conference calls and meetings at the office already scheduled for the 8th and 9th, I knew I couldn't leave for Canada until the 10th. Willie and the Dirt Band were playing in Sydney on the 11th.

After literally hours of searching, by Saturday night I had managed to find a way to get myself to Sydney on the morning of the 11th. Unfortunately, my first flight would be taking off from Los Angeles on the morning of the 10th. It would take two days, four separate flights, and four different time zones to get there, but I had gotten myself booked, and that was all that mattered.

In the early morning hours of the 7th, I shot off another email to John, letting him know that I'd booked a one-way trip to Sydney and asking him where he'd be staying while there. He wrote back, "One way? Planning on staying?"

He had a good point. If it took me an entire day to figure out how to get there, who knew how long it'd take me to figure out how to get back home? I made a mental note to call a travel agent first thing Monday morning.

The rest of John's email was the tour itinerary:

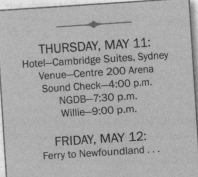

THURSDAY, MAY 11:
Hotel—Cambridge Suites, Sydney
Venue—Centre 200 Arena
Sound Check—4:00 p.m.
NGDB—7:30 p.m.
Willie—9:00 p.m.

FRIDAY, MAY 12:
Ferry to Newfoundland . . .

~LEAP! YOU CAN~ ALWAYS LOOK LATER

Not all of my advice is for the faint of heart. If you haven't figured it out by now, I'll just come right out and say it: song plugging is not for the meek. The Bible says the meek shall inherit the earth. In the meantime, those of us in the music business shall do what we can to keep the earth moving, shaking, dancing, and romancing to our songs until the meek ones' inheritance comes due.

When I was a kid, one of my grade-school teachers shook her finger at me and said, "You've got to learn to be more careful. Always remember to look before you leap." I thought it was the funniest thing I'd ever heard—especially since I thought she'd said, "Look before you *leak*." But I digress . . .

Of course, what my teacher meant was that I should always consider the possible consequences of my actions in advance. Granted it's good advice—but I'm glad I didn't listen.

I moved from Alabama to New York City on a bus, with just enough money to get by for a few weeks. I finally managed to get a job in the music business, only to write a commentary in *Billboard* that resulted in the need to search for a new job. That new job led to my meeting Jerry Leiber and Mike Stoller—which eventually led to my running one of the biggest independent music publishing companies in the country. In all of those years, I never once considered the consequences of my actions in advance. It sounds crazy, but it's true.

If you're going to be a doctor or a lawyer or an accountant, or work in any profession that's filled with rules and guidelines, you have to learn to do things by the book. But if you're going to be in the creative end of the music business, you're going to have to take the occasional leap without looking down before you jump.

Ferry to Newfoundland! What the hell? I pulled out my world atlas and took a long look at Canada. Sure enough: Newfoundland wasn't attached to Nova Scotia—something anybody who knew much about geography would already be well aware of. The map showed a pretty large body of water separating the two, with a dotted line indicating the ferry route from Sydney to something called Channel-Port aux Basques. As if that weren't bad enough, Corner Brook—where Willie's next gig was on the 13th—was over 100 miles from Channel-Port aux Basques. I'd been so proud of myself for figuring out how to get from LA to Sydney. Now I had to book a ferryboat and a rental car.

I went back to the Internet in search of ferries to Newfoundland. Luckily, there was only one ferry company that made the daily trip from North Sydney to Channel-Port aux Basques. I called the number for Marine Atlantic in North Sydney and spoke to a nice lady who booked my round-trip voyage. Since she was being so friendly, I asked her if she could recommend a rental car service. "Oh, that would be Tony," she said. "Here's his phone number."

I put in a call to Tony, at which point I discovered that people in Newfoundland have an accent unlike anything I'd ever heard. Tony sounded like a combination of Prince Charles, Keith Richards, and Bono, and he talked faster than the guy who does the legal disclaimer at the end of car commercials. I had no idea what he was saying. I just gave him my arrival date and my departure date and hoped for the best.

ENGINE ALTERNATOR

C. PROPELLER

MASTER UNIT
SPEED CONTROL
LINKAGE

SYNCHRONIZER
MASTER UNIT

SWITCH
PANEL

BATTERY

JUNCTION BOX

VOLTAGE BOOSTER

TYPICAL DISPOSITION OF UNITS & CONDUIT

INSTALLATION DIAGRAM

CHAPTER THIRTY-SEVEN

When I got to the office on Monday morning, May 8th, I called a travel agent and told her my situation. I needed her to book a one-way trip back to Los Angeles from Sydney, Nova Scotia, for the following Monday. My plan was to arrive in Sydney on Thursday, May 11th, pitch the song to Willie sometime during the next couple of days, take the ferry from Newfoundland back to Nova Scotia on the 14th, and then be on a plane heading back toward LA on the 15th. In less than a half hour she called me back with my entire return itinerary. It had taken me an entire day to figure out how to get there. It took her less than thirty minutes to figure out how to get me back home. As soon as I got off the phone with the travel agent, I made a silent pledge to myself that in the future, I would focus on doing only those things I know how to do well and would entrust others with the task of doing everything else.

My next job was to burn two CDs of the Sinatra Song, print the lyrics out on Leiber & Stoller Music Publishing letterhead (two copies), and also take two copies of the lead sheet. Since presentation is such an important part of song plugging, at L&S we have CD booklet inserts with the company logo printed on the front and all of our contact information printed on the back. Before I slid the inserts into the CD cases, I had Jerry and Mike write a personal message to Willie and sign both of them.

Why two copies of everything? Luggage can get lost. Briefcases can be stolen. With one copy in my briefcase and one copy in my suitcase, I knew the odds of losing both before getting to Canada would be greatly reduced.

The rest of Monday and all day Tuesday were a blur. I'd been pitching songs for decades—sometimes traveling as far as Nashville—but venturing all the way across Canada in an effort to pitch a single song was a first. At least when I was going to Nashville I'd always had all of my appointments set up in advance. This time, in the words of an old World War II song, I'd be "comin' in on a wing and a prayer"—and a ferryboat and a rental car.

CHAPTER THIRTY-EIGHT

The first leg of my trip to Sydney, Nova Scotia, took off from Los Angeles International Airport on the morning of May 10th. Three flights later—a few minutes before midnight—I landed in Halifax. My flight to Sydney wouldn't be leaving until early the next morning. To my pleasant surprise, there was an actual station where I could set up my laptop on a small table, pull up a chair, and try to stay awake until I heard the boarding call for the Sydney flight.

Most people in my situation would be either going to a hotel or curling up in one of the terminal's nice, soft cushiony chairs to catch a few hours' sleep. No, that's not quite accurate. Most people wouldn't find themselves in my situation. That night in Halifax, as I sat staring at the upside-down apple on my closed laptop, I realized that I was, without question, the *only* person in the history of the universe in my particular situation. I also realized for the first time that this was probably the most ridiculous thing I'd ever done. Up until that moment, I'd been so busy getting the whole trip put together that I hadn't begun to see the folly of this endeavor until I was sitting there, all alone, in an airport terminal in Nova Scotia.

One thing was certain: I wasn't going to be curling up in one of those soft, cushiony chairs. This mission was now officially under way, and the last thing I wanted to do at this point was to wake up just in time to see my plane taxiing down the runway without me on it.

My plan that night had been to continue working on the Duane Allman biography. The deadline for the completed manuscript to be turned in to my editor was only weeks away. I couldn't let a little thing like a wild goose chase across Canada in search of Willie Nelson get in the way of a book deadline, so I opened my laptop, fully intending to write about Duane's influence on the work of the band Lynyrd Skynyrd; about how the band had recorded the song "Free Bird" in honor of the fallen guitarist they idolized; and about how they performed the song at every concert, always dedicating it to "Brother Duane."

And then I remembered that Lynyrd Skynyrd's plane had crashed in a forest near Gillsburg, Mississippi, killing two members of the band, a backup singer, an assistant road manager, the pilot, and the copilot. I looked up from my keyboard, stared at the planes lined up out on the tarmac, and decided this might be a good night to take a break from working on the book.

As I watched the planes taking off into the sky, my mind drifted to Kris Kristofferson landing his helicopter on Johnny Cash's lawn. I thought about Lou Levy paying fifty cents a day for an elevator operator to sing "Shoe Shine Boy." I'd been in the music business a long time, and I'd heard a lot of song plugging stories during those years. Some of them were true, and some of them were most likely pure apocrypha.

One of the complaints I've heard from the few remaining "old-timers" in the music industry (and yes, I'm talking about people even older than I am) is that there aren't any great characters left in this business any more. When they say "characters," what they're usually referring to are those seemingly larger-than-life men and women who had powerful personalities, great senses of humor, and an appetite for the good life. The caricature is a finely tailored, overweight man with one hand holding a cigar and the other hand in a songwriter's pocket. These were mainly New Yorkers—men and women who generally made frequent trips to the racetrack, were known to consume dark liquor, always wore the latest fashions, and had the entrepreneurial flair it took to run an independent record label, an indie music publishing company, or both.

One of those characters was a one-time business partner of Leiber and Stoller's named George Goldner. A man who ran dance halls in New York and New Jersey, Goldner became a fan of Latin music, leading to the formation of his first label, Tico Records, in the late 1940s. He signed artists such as Tito Puente and had great success in the Latin market.

Next, Goldner started a second label called Rama, focusing on R&B acts such as the

Turn Me Loose: The Songs of Pomus & Shuman— That's Doc Pomus on the right.

Crows. When the Crows had a major hit called "Gee," Goldner formed a third label that he named after the Crows' hit. When Frankie Lymon and the Teenagers scored a Top 10 pop/No. 1 R&B smash on Gee Records with "Why Do Fools Fall in Love," Goldner seemed to have the Midas touch.

But soon, he had sold a 50 percent interest in all three labels to Joe Kolsky, a business partner of yet another music business character named Morris Levy. Together the three men, along with Phil Khals, formed Roulette Records, and quickly began scoring hits with Buddy Knox ("Party Doll"), Ronnie Hawkins ("Forty Days"), and others.

And in almost no time, *Billboard* announced that Goldner had sold all of his interest in Roulette, as well as his remaining interests in Tico, Rama, and Gee, to Morris Levy and partners.

As Jerry Leiber once succinctly put it, "Word was that Goldner was hooked on the horses."

Somehow, George remained in the game. After selling all of his earlier labels to Levy, Goldner formed End Records, quickly having yet another hit with "He's Gone" by the Chantels. Naturally, he named his next label Gone, and watched "Could This Be Magic" by the Dubs go flying up the charts. Then came Little Anthony and the Imperials with "Tears On My Pillow" and "Shimmy, Shimmy, Ko-Ko-Bop." It seemed that no one in the business had ears more golden than Goldner.

But in the early 1960s, End and Gone went the way of Tico, Rama, and Gee—straight into the hands and pockets of Morris Levy.

One evening in 1963, Old Town Records owner Hy Weiss introduced Jerry Leiber to George Goldner at a steakhouse/music business hangout called Al and Dick's. Even though Hy Weiss claimed Goldner was broke, the former label own-er still dressed like a prince: black silk pin-striped suit, gold cufflinks, diamond stickpin—Goldner never let a few losses at the track affect his wardrobe budget.

The meeting that night resulted in Goldner becoming Leiber and Stoller's partner in a label they called Red Bird Records. In no time, Red Bird released its first hit, "Chapel of Love" by the Dixie Cups. Even with a succession of bestsell-ing records by groups such as the Dixie Cups, the Shangri-Las, the Ad-Libs, and others, Leiber and Stoller soon grew nervous about the company Goldner was keeping. In fact, when one of George's acquaintances informed Leiber that he was now one of Red Bird's new partners, Jerry realized that the rumors about where Goldner was getting his wardrobe and track money were true.

Leiber and Stoller soon parted ways with Goldner, selling him Red Bird Re-cords for a dollar. And even with a label at his disposal that had amassed dozens of hits, Goldner's luck finally ran out. He eventually sold Red Bird—although this time, not to Morris Levy—and passed away at fifty-two.

When I once asked Jerry how Goldner could have such an incredible talent for hearing and predicting so many hit records, he told me, "Because George had the musical taste of a fourteen-year-old girl."

A lot of the songwriters from those days were great characters too. When I was still with the Songwriters Hall of Fame, I had the pleasure of meeting and getting to know quite a few of them. One of my favorites was Doc Pomus. He and his songwriting partner, Mort Shuman, wrote the hits "This Magic Moment," "Viva Las Vegas," "I Count the Tears," and many others. Doc had polio as a child, which resulted in his using crutches to get around for much of his life. By the time I met him in the early 1980s, he was confined to a wheelchair. He wasn't able to use his legs, but he didn't have any problem using his telephone. Doc and I ended up being phone buddies. If I was having a bad day at work, getting a call from Doc would always make things better. During the last years of his life, I came to find out that Doc had dozens of phone buddies. But I wasn't jealous. He, too, was one of those larger-than-life guys—literally, in his case—so there was plenty of him to go around.

One of the many things I admired about Doc Pomus was that—to the very end of his life—he never stopped writing songs. Some songwriters get complacent or bogged down in business details. Some simply seem to lose their hunger to write. But not Doc. He would frequently call to tell me about a song he'd recently written and who had just cut it. But he was also good at reminiscing about the "old days." (According to Doc, the old days were back when all the focus was on writing a good song and making a good record—as opposed to seeing who could make the most money.) One day Doc called to tell me about when he and Mort Shuman wrote "Save the Last Dance for Me." Doc and Mort would frequently send songs to Leiber and Stoller, because in those days, Jerry and Mike were producing a lot of acts for Atlantic Records. (Once again, truth is stranger than fiction. At the time Doc told me this story, I had no clue I'd be going to work for L&S one day.) As was often the case, Pomus and Shuman sent Leiber and Stoller their two latest songs—"Save the Last Dance for Me" and "Nobody But Me." The year was 1960.

Shortly after Doc and Mort sent the two songs to Leiber and Stoller, Doc got a call from a Louisiana-based singer named Jimmy Clanton. Jimmy had recently scored a million-selling single called "Just a Dream." He'd been on *American Bandstand*, and he'd been touring with guys like Jerry Lee Lewis and Fats Domino. Jimmy told Doc that he was in town, looking for a follow-up hit. Naturally, Doc and Mort played him one of their most recent songs—"Save the Last Dance for Me." Jimmy knew a hit when he heard one, so he told the guys he was going into the studio to cut it.

At this point in his phone call to me, I heard Doc start laughing. He said,

"And wouldn't you know it, just as Jimmy is getting ready to go into the studio, Jerry Leiber calls to tell me that he and Mike Stoller are also about to go into the studio—with the Drifters—to cut both 'Save the Last Dance for Me' *and* 'Nobody But Me.' Jimmy Clanton was a nice singer, but the Drifters were *huge!*"

(Most of us, and that includes me, weren't even born when the Drifters had their first hit in 1953. But even if you're too young to have heard their recordings except when your grandmother was listening to the oldies station—or even if you've never heard of the Drifters at all—you've no doubt heard some of the songs that they made famous: "There Goes My Baby," "Up on the Roof," "On Broadway," "Under the Boardwalk," and so forth.)

I knew that the Drifters ended up having a major hit with "Save the Last Dance For Me," so I asked Doc what he did about poor Jimmy Clanton. He said,

> Well, we would've pitched him 'Nobody But Me,' but Mike and Jerry had taken that one too. Then I remembered a song we'd written for Bobby Rydell called "Go, Bobby, Go." In fact, he'd recorded it, but it hadn't been released, and it was probably never going to get released, so I went back to Jimmy and told him that Mort and I had written a song especially for him called "Go, Jimmy, Go." Well, he really loved the idea, so he forgot all about the other song and cut "Go, Jimmy, Go" instead.

Now *that's* song plugging. By the time the dust settled, the Drifters' recording of "Save the Last Dance for Me" had hit the top of the charts. And while the Drifters' single was finally heading back down the charts, Jimmy Clanton's recording of "Go, Jimmy, Go" was on its way up, eventually landing in the Top 5.

Doc Pomus would go on to have his songs recorded by everyone from Ray Charles to John Lennon to Robert Plant to Bruce Springsteen to Elvis Presley.

When it comes to song plugging tales, just about everyone who was lucky enough to have a song recorded by Elvis seems to have a good one to tell about how the King of rock & roll came to record his or her tune. In reality, for much of his career, Elvis would listen to the acetates song plugger Freddy Bienstock would deliver to him and then pick out the ones he liked. Or when it came to his movies, a songwriting team was usually assigned to come up with songs that fit specific scenes in the script.

That wasn't the case for Elvis's recording of "Too Much." In fact, when Lee Rosenberg and Bernard Weinman wrote the song, they weren't even thinking about pitching it to Elvis. They did manage to get several artists you never heard of to record it—singers such as Bernard Hardison, Judy Tremaine, and Frankie Castro. Needless to say, nothing happened with any of those records. But the two writers still believed in the song, and when Lee Rosenberg heard that Elvis Presley was going to be taking a train from Nashville to Hollywood, he decided to make his move. On the day Elvis was scheduled to make his long train ride across the country, Lee grabbed a copy of the Bernard Hardison recording of "Too Much" and headed for the depot. When Elvis arrived, Lee was there. He introduced himself to Presley, handed him the record, and hoped for the best. Luckily for Rosenberg and Weinman, Elvis always kept a portable turntable with him. On the long trip west, Elvis had plenty of time to listen to the record—and he liked what he heard. When he went into the studio in September of 1956, he recorded "Too Much" as one of the four songs on the session.

In January of 1957, "Too Much" was released as a single. And then the fates smiled upon Rosenberg and Weinman. The same week the single was released, Elvis went on *The Ed Sullivan Show*. Elvis Presley had been on Sullivan's show before. In fact, it was his first appearance on Sullivan the previous year that had caused the singer to rocket to stardom. But *this* show—on January 6, 1957—was the infamous appearance in which the cameramen were ordered to shoot Elvis from the waist up only, due to all the controversy that had begun to swirl around about the fact that Elvis swiveled his hips way too much for the conservative folks of 1950s America. Naturally, that caused the kids of all those conservative parents to run out and buy the single of the new song Elvis had performed that night, sending "Too Much" to the top of the charts.

Two more songs recorded by Elvis were "Separate Ways" and "Always On My Mind." Written by Johnny Christopher, Mark James, and Wayne Carson, "Always On My Mind" was a song Elvis learned about from Red West. The multitalented West was one of Elvis's entourage—the group of guys known as the Memphis Mafia. Not only was he Elvis's friend and bodyguard, Red West was also an actor and songwriter.

In December of 1971, Priscilla Presley had let Elvis know that she was leaving him. Over the next few months, Elvis recorded a body of work that perfectly captured the events unfolding in his life. Knowing his friend's state of mind, Red wrote the lyrics to "Separate Ways" with composer Richard Mainegra. After Elvis agreed to record "Separate Ways," West played "Always On My Mind" for the singer. Red had heard Wayne Carson's recording of the song and knew that it also captured the feelings Elvis still had for Priscilla. Elvis recorded both songs in March of 1972, along with others in a similar vein, including "For the Good Times" and "Where Do I Go from Here." In November of that year, RCA released its latest Elvis Presley single, with "Separate Ways" on one side and "Always on My Mind" on the other. "Separate Ways" became a Top 20 pop hit, while "Always on My Mind" became a Top 20 hit on the country charts—resulting in yet another in a very long line of million-selling singles for Elvis.

A decade later, Willie Nelson and Merle Haggard were in the studio recording the tracks for what would become the album *Pancho & Lefty*. "Always On My Mind" cowriter Johnny Christopher was a guitarist on the sessions, so he took the opportunity to pitch the song to Merle. When the Hag didn't appear particularly interested in cutting the tune, Willie told Christopher, "That's for me." Unfamiliar with Presley's recording of the song, Nelson would later say he was "bowled over" by the song from the moment he heard Johnny Christopher play it for Merle Haggard.

Immediately after the duet sessions with Merle concluded, Willie went back into the studio with *Pancho & Lefty*'s producer—Chips Moman—as well as many of that album's same musicians, including Johnny Christopher. By 1982, Willie Nelson was already a major star, both as a singer and actor—but with the release of the album *Always On My Mind*—Willie reached the pinnacle of his recording success.

The single release of the title song topped the country charts, as did the album. "Always On My Mind" also reached No. 5 on the pop charts, eventually becoming a platinum-selling single. Meanwhile, the album sold over 4 million copies, as well as spinning off two more hit singles.

When awards season came around, "Always On My Mind" garnered a Grammy for Nelson in the "Best Country Vocal Performance, Male" category; a Grammy for Christopher, James, and Carson in the "Best Country Song" category; and yet another Grammy for the three writers when it was named "Song

"Always On My Mind" remained in the No. 1 spot on the country charts for more than twenty weeks. The album's title song garnered Grammy Awards for Best Country Song; Best Country Vocal Performance, Male; and Song of the Year.

of the Year." The Country Music Association also named it "Song of the Year," as well as "Single of the Year." In 2008, Willie's recording of "Always On My Mind" was inducted into the Grammy Hall of Fame—and it all happened thanks to Johnny Christopher pitching his song to Merle Haggard while Willie Nelson was in the same room.

In addition to Willie Nelson and others, my friend Roger Deitz once interviewed Arlo Guthrie for *Acoustic Guitar* magazine. During the interview, Arlo told Roger this song plugging story:

> I was playing in a club in Chicago called the Quiet Knight in 1971. The owner, Richard Harding, was a friend of mine. He wanted me to listen to a song by a local buddy of his. I said I didn't want to hear any songs. I was tired and I wanted to go to the hotel.
>
> So, this little guy comes walking up to the bar and says, "Arlo, I just want to sing you one song." So I answered, "Well, if you buy me a beer, I'll sit here and drink it—and as long as it lasts, you can do whatever you want."

It turned out to be one of the finer beers of my career. The guy
was Steve Goodman, and his song [was] "City of New Orleans."

Although Arlo is best known for his self-penned eighteen-minute opus "Al-
ice's Restaurant," Steve Goodman's composition about the "disappearing railroad
blues" became a Top 20 hit for Guthrie in 1972—the highest-charting single of
his career.

The song would go on to be recorded by dozens of performers, including
John Denver, Judy Collins, Johnny Cash, and—why not?—Willie Nelson. The
title song of Willie's 1984 platinum-selling album, "City Of New Orleans" was
released as a single that summer, chugging to the top of the country charts and
becoming Nelson's twelfth No. 1 hit.

~ THERE'S MORE THAN ONE WAY TO SKIN A CAT ~

As far as the song pluggers in this chapter are concerned, Doc Pomus and Mort Shuman used a couple of different methods. They submitted "Save the Last Dance for Me" and "Nobody But Me" to Leiber and Stoller—two record producers they knew personally, who they also knew were always on the lookout for great songs. In your quest to get to know everyone you can in the music business, record producers should be high on your list. The more producers you know, the better your chances of getting your songs recorded.

In the case of Doc and Mort's pitch to Jimmy Clanton, they adapted a preexisting song to fit a specific artist. If you're a songwriter, you might want to accept the idea that flexibility isn't a bad thing. I've known plenty of songwriters who adamantly refuse to change a single word or a single note because they consider what they've written to be works of great art that, once written, are locked in stone. Those kind of songwriters fall into two distinct categories: 1) Songwriters who are so monumentally successful that artists will agree to perform their songs exactly as written, and 2) Songwriters who haven't ever had any of their songs recorded because they're too damn stubborn to allow what they've written to be changed in any way. Unless you already fall into category number 1, you might want to get off of your high horse and be flexible—unless you'd prefer to fall into category number 2.

Lee Rosenberg, the cowriter of "Too Much," went with the "right place, right time" approach. Once again, unless you've already written quite a few hits, recording artists, record producers, artist managers, and the like aren't going to beat a path to your door. You've got to go where they are. Metaphorically speaking, Elvis has left the train station, but there are plenty of artists who are still alive and well and looking for potential hit songs to record. Back in the days when we were all pitching songs via cassette tape, I once found myself in the same room with a very famous R&B vocal group. I had just signed a song to my publishing company that day, and I still had the cassette of the song in my pocket. By the time the well-known R&B group left the room, that cassette was in the lead singer's pocket. I'd never met them before—and they certainly had no clue who I was—but I wasn't about to miss out on a song plugging opportunity. As much as I've continually emphasized the importance of getting to know everyone you can in the music business, you should never pass up an opportunity to pitch a song just because you haven't been formally introduced. Elvis Presley had no idea who Lee Rosenberg was, but he was stuck on a cross-country train ride, so he listened to Lee's song. If you're in the right place at the right time, pitch away.

When Red West wrote the lyrics to "Separate Ways," he was writing the song for someone he knew well—well enough that he knew the current frame of mind of the artist he was writing the song for. In our world of twenty-four-hour news networks, daily gossip shows, and Internet sites such as tmz.com, we're all constantly being subjected to the goings-on of performers almost in real time. Even though you might not know a particular recording artist personally, you can pretty much guess that artist's frame of mind from what *Entertainment Tonight* reported about her last night. Sure, it's kind of creepy and perhaps a wee bit underhanded, but if you've got a song that you feel perfectly encapsulates what that artist is probably feeling right now, there's no better time to pitch that song than right now.

When Johnny Christopher pitched "Always On My Mind" to Merle Haggard, he was just plain lucky that Willie Nelson was in the room while he was pitching the tune to Hag. But at least Johnny wasn't shy. He was a studio guitarist taking the golden opportunity to promote one of his songs face-to-face with an artist he believed his song was right for. If someone asked me to pick the perfect place for song plugging, I'd say there is no perfect place, but the recording studio is a pretty ideal spot. You don't have to be a studio musician to be there. You don't have to be the recording engineer either. You just have to be there.

I've always loved Arlo Guthrie's story of how Steve Goodman pitched him "City of New Orleans." There's a good chance Arlo might've passed up the opportunity to hear the song if Goodman had approached him directly. But Steve Goodman had wisely chosen to use an emissary, club owner Richard Harding, who was a friend of Arlo's. (And of course, he was also wise to buy Arlo a beer.) Goodman also knew the song he'd written was a perfect match for Arlo. Even though Willie Nelson's version was a huge hit, "City of New Orleans" will always be associated with Arlo Guthrie, first and foremost. I'll freely admit that it's pretty difficult to get a song directly to a major recording act. Getting access to a friend of that artist is usually much easier. If pitching a song through an artist's friend seems cringe-worthy to you, you need to change your mind-set. You're not taking advantage of that artist's friend. You're giving that artist's friend the opportunity to tell everyone he knows that he's the guy who was responsible for hooking up his recording artist friend with your song.

CHAPTER THIRTY-NINE

I landed in Sydney, Nova Scotia, and took a cab to the Cambridge Suites Hotel. When I checked in, I left a message for John McEuen, letting him know that I'd arrived.

We met up that afternoon and took a taxi to Centre 200—home of the Cape Breton Screaming Eagles hockey team. Our first job was to find the Dirt Band's dressing room, which was easy enough since there was a sign on the door that said "Nitty Gritty Dirt Band Dressing Room." It could have as easily said "Visiting Team's Locker Room," because that's exactly what it was.

On the road, everything is temporary. There were paper signs taped on doors for Willie's dressing room, Willie's band's dressing room, the tour's production office, and my personal favorite, "Willie Nelson Tuning Room." I was aware that Willie's well-worn guitar, Trigger, was one of the best known guitars in the world, but until that day, I had no idea it got its own room to be tuned in.

When John and I walked into the production office, he introduced me to the two young women who were in charge of coordinating everything a tour of this magnitude requires. They gave me a backstage pass for that night's show, and then John and I headed toward the stage for the Dirt Band's sound check.

When it's a hockey rink, Centre 200 holds around 5,000 hockey fans. When it's a concert hall, 1,500 folding chairs are added to the mix. I chose a folding chair in the center of the room and became an audience of one, watching and listening as the band tested microphones and amplifiers to

The poster for Willie's Canadian tour, with "special guests" the Nitty Gritty Dirt Band.

make sure everything was in order for that night's show. As they ran through a couple of songs that afternoon, I was fifteen years old again (or perhaps more accurately—still).

With sound check over, John and I headed toward the catering room. As we were strolling down the hall, I saw Poodie Locke and Mickey Raphael—Willie's harmonica player—walking toward us. Mickey and I had actually met and conversed on a few occasions in the past. We didn't know each other well, but he knew me well enough to know that he shouldn't be expecting to bump into me at a hockey rink in Nova Scotia. Always laid back and cool, Mickey smiled and asked, "What are you doing here?"

"Well, you're going to think I'm crazy," I said, "But I've got this Sinatra recording of a song Leiber and Stoller want me to pitch to Willie . . ."

Before I could finish my story, Poodie jumped in. "Man, you *are* crazy." He was laughing as he said it, but I was hard-pressed to disagree. Despite Poodie's rather accurate assessment of the situation, Mickey seemed at least mildly impressed. "If you're going to be around for a few days, you'll probably get a chance to play it for him," he said. I thanked Mickey for his words of encouragement, and then John and I continued toward the catering room.

~ WHERE NEVER IS HEARD A DISCOURAGING WORD ~

When Poodie Locke told me I was crazy, I knew he wasn't being negative or trying to discourage me. He was just giving me his honest reaction to the idea that anyone would go to such lengths to pitch a song. Nobody ever said you have to be totally sane to be a song plugger, so I took Poodie's words as an affirmation of what I already knew: I truly was crazy to fly all the way across Canada to try to pitch the Sinatra Song to Willie Nelson—but I was going to give it my best shot anyway.

Poodie was known throughout the music business as an honest, positive, upbeat person. He was also known for his slogan "There are no bad days." Over the years though, I've come across a lot of folks in the music business who seem to think most days are bad. I've never understood why anyone lucky enough to be surrounded by music every day would be so pessimistic. Would they prefer to be surrounded by the sound of squawking turkeys? Thanks to that summer job I once had at a poultry plant, I can assure you that—given a choice—music is the more pleasant option.

As a song plugger, you have to stay upbeat. If you truly believe in your songs, never let yourself be discouraged by what others say. As a songwriter, it can be pretty difficult to determine the quality of your own work. If someone you really respect—someone you believe to be an excellent judge of what makes a great song—should tell you that one of your songs needs work, ask them to be specific. They might be able to give you the kind of advice that can turn a good song into a great one.

Earlier I told you about how the song "Jackson" came to be recorded by Johnny Cash and June Carter. Since 1967, it's been cut by numerous acts and has been used in both television shows and motion pictures. CMT, the country music TV network, ranked it at No. 4 on its list of country's 100 Greatest Duets.

If Billy Edd Wheeler hadn't played his original version of "Jackson" for Jerry Leiber, chances are it never would have been recorded at all. When Jerry heard the song, he told Billy Edd, "Your first few verses don't work. Throw them away and start the song with your last verse." Luckily, Billy Edd knew Jerry Leiber to be a pretty good judge of what makes a great song. So the last verse became the first verse, and as Billy Edd says, "Thanks to Jerry's editing and help, it worked."

It not only worked—it turned out to be one of country music's most enduring duets. When someone you truly respect gives you constructive criticism, don't think of his or her comments as being discouraging words. Listen closely. They might be words that could change your life.

CHAPTER FORTY

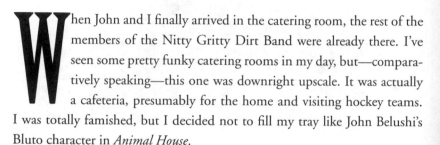

When John and I finally arrived in the catering room, the rest of the members of the Nitty Gritty Dirt Band were already there. I've seen some pretty funky catering rooms in my day, but—comparatively speaking—this one was downright upscale. It was actually a cafeteria, presumably for the home and visiting hockey teams. I was totally famished, but I decided not to fill my tray like John Belushi's Bluto character in *Animal House*.

After going through the chow line, I took my sparsely filled plate and sat down next to Jeff Hanna. His first words to me were "Hey, Randy. Is that all you're going to eat?"

I had no idea how he knew my name, but I decided to do my best to make a good first impression. "Well, Jeff, now that you mention it, I think there's still some room on this plate." I stood up, went back to the food line, and told the ladies behind the counter to give me an extra helping of everything. When I sat back down with every inch of my tray covered in food, the ice was broken.

I knew about the Dirt Band's musical history, but John was the only member of the group I'd spent any time with until that afternoon. Not surprisingly, I found each of the guys to have a great sense of humor. After so many years together, they'd have to.

The Nitty Gritty Dirt Band formed in May of 1966 in Southern California. The following year, their debut album was released. As had been the case with Willie, it looked as if they were on their way when their very first single, "Buy for Me the Rain," became a Top 40 hit. Then came their second,

Uncle Charlie & His Dog Teddy— The Nitty Gritty Dirt Band's 1970 breakthrough album.

third, and fourth albums, with not another charting single among them. As had also been the case with Willie, the band refused to be discouraged by a lack of chart action.

Then, in 1970, *Uncle Charlie & His Dog Teddy*—their *fifth* album—was released. The record's first single, "Mr. Bojangles," was a smash. By 2006, there had been twenty-five more albums and dozens of hit singles. The personnel had undergone a few shakeups over the course of four decades, but as we sat around the table at the Centre 200 arena cafeteria in Sydney, Nova Scotia, that May afternoon, three of the four members of the band were the same guys who had recorded that first album back in 1967. Bob Carpenter—the most recent addition—had already been in the band for over twenty-five years.

I did my best not to pepper the guys with questions, since I knew I wouldn't be asking them anything they hadn't been asked a thousand times before. Mainly I just listened, getting to know each of them individually.

I learned that Jeff Hanna now lived in Nashville—his wife the very talented

~ BE VEWY, VEWY QUIET ~

I've offered a lot of advice throughout this book, and I hope that some of my suggestions turn out to be helpful to you during a long and successful career. Now I'd like to let you in on a little secret that might not only be advantageous to you as a song plugger but might actually change your life. I know this might sound rude, but don't take it personally. (Remember: heart of a poet—skin of a rhino.) Okay, here it is: people would rather hear themselves talk than listen to what you have to say.

It's a fact of life, so don't fight it. It doesn't matter if you have the oration skills of Patrick Henry: if someone else is talking, your job is to stay as quiet as a mime in a soundproof box. Do not interrupt; do not interject; do not disturb. Let the other party speak. And while he or she is talking, don't be thinking about what your response is going to be. If the other party is speaking, do nothing but absorb the words being spoken.

The best way to pitch a song is to let the song pitch itself. Don't start talking the second the song ends. (Much of the time you'll be lucky if the song even gets to the end without the other party hitting the stop button.) Let the person listening to the song react. If you're in a meeting with a record producer who says he doesn't think the song is right for his artist, it's highly unlikely you're going to be able to convince him otherwise. If the producer says it's a great song but it's not right for his artist, ask him who he hears singing it. No need to walk away from the meeting without accomplishing something. He might have a strong opinion about who your song is right for. He might even be able to tell you the best way to get the song to that artist.

But let's think positively for a moment. If the producer says he thinks the song is perfect for his act, then you can talk—but not a lot. Thank him. Make sure he has all of your contact info and that you have all of his. If he wants to pontificate on how he envisions the song being produced, listen to what he's saying. Once he's finished talking, thank him again and get the hell out. Once you've made the sale, absolutely no good can come from sticking around and taking the chance of overstaying your welcome.

Back when tribute albums were all the rage, a noted music veteran and I went to visit the president of a major record label. The concept was simple: we had an idea for a tribute album that would primarily feature artists signed to the record label we were pitching the concept to.

Within five minutes, the president of the label had already started matching songs from the catalog I represented to artists on his roster. He was clearly enthusiastic about the idea. I could tell we had him hooked. The catch had been made—but then we let him wriggle off the line. The meeting should have lasted ten minutes, but the noted music veteran I'd brought with me to help pitch the idea couldn't stop talking. Maybe he was nervous. Maybe he was overly excited. What he started sounding like was a desperate man begging for his life.

Twenty minutes into the meeting, the label president's eyes started to glaze over. I knew we were losing him, so I made my move. When all else fails, stand up. I looked at my watch and jumped out of my chair. I shook the president's hand and thanked him for his time. My colleague remained seated and kept talking. Then the president of the label stood up. Finally, the noted music veteran got the picture and stood up too. But by then it was too late. I could see it in the label president's face. He was so turned off by my associate that he'd already made the decision he didn't want to work with him.

When I got back to the office, one of my coworkers asked me how the meeting had gone. I said, "We talked the head of the label into doing the project, and then—in less than a half-hour—we talked him right back out of it."

Be enthusiastic. Be positive. Be friendly. Be professional. But above all else, be quiet.

songwriter Matraca Berg. I found out that Jimmie Fadden was based in Florida and—like John McEuen—had been a close friend of Duane Allman's. Bob Carpenter and I discovered we had several mutual friends, since he too lives in LA. John, of course, was already a good pal. On the surface, the four of them seemed to have very little in common aside from the music they'd made. But all four had lived through the highs and lows and in-betweens of life as an American band. They had toured the world time and again—and this time, for a handful of days, I got to experience the adventure with them.

CHAPTER FORTY-ONE

Getting to see and hear the Nitty Gritty Dirt Band in concert for the first time since I was a teenager reminded me why I'd gotten into this business in the first place: it's all about the music, and there's nothing better than hearing and seeing a great band going full throttle, live and in person. These guys were real musicians, playing real instruments, singing real songs—all four of them looking like they were having the times of their lives every second they were onstage at the Centre 200 arena in Sydney, Nova Scotia.

In the late 1960s, the Nitty Gritty Dirt Band had been at the very forefront of the country rock movement—preceding the Flying Burrito Brothers, the Eagles, Poco, and Pure Prairie League—and they still remained true to their country rock roots while somehow managing to change with the times just enough to never sound outdated.

Following the Top 10 pop chart success of "Mr. Bojangles" in 1970, the band's 1972 three-record set of traditional country music, *Will the Circle Be Unbroken*, went platinum. Although the band continued to score occasional pop hits throughout the 1970s with singles such as "An American Dream," most of their singles hovered in the bottom half of the Top 100. "Make a Little Magic" went as high as No. 25 in 1980—and then the pop hits stopped.

Having had a grand total of three Top 40 singles on the pop charts since 1967, by the early 1980s it was starting to look as if the band's best days might be behind them. As it turned out, however, nothing could be further from the truth.

Even though the members of the Dirt Band were still making the kind

The Nitty Gritty Dirt Band—1973 lineup (L-R) John McEuen, Les Thompson, Jimmie Ibbotson, Jimmie Fadden, and Jeff Hanna.

of music that had brought them success on the pop charts, their last two hits—"An American Dream" and "Make a Little Magic"—had both made a little noise on country radio too. In 1983, that noise got a whole lot louder. That year, the band's single "Dance Little Jean" was a Top 10 hit on the country charts. Their next one, "Long Hard Road (The Sharecropper's Dream)," went all the way to the top. Throughout the decade of the 1980s, the Nitty Gritty Dirt Band proved to be a country music juggernaut. "I Love Only You," "High Horse," "Modern Day Romance," "Home Again in My Heart," "Partners, Brothers, and Friends," "Stand a Little Rain," "Fire in the Sky," "Baby's Got a Hold on Me," "Fishin' in the Dark," "Oh What a Love," "Workin' Man (Nowhere to Go)," "I've Been Lookin'," and "Down That Road Tonight" were all Top 10 country hits—many of which went to No. 1.

Their 1986 "Greatest Hits" album, *Twenty Years of Dirt*, went platinum. So did their 1989 album, *Will the Circle Be Unbroken: Volume Two*. The band won three Grammy Awards for tracks appearing on the second *Circle* album, which also won "Album of the Year" honors from the Country Music Association.

Although the decade of the '80s might be considered the band's most successful—particularly considering the volume of hits they recorded during those years—the group continued to make quality music in the decades that followed. Throughout the ensuing years, they continued to tour, made new records, and received more CMA and Grammy nominations, as well as yet another Grammy Award.

By the time I caught up with the Dirt Band in Canada in 2006, they had reached a status not dissimilar to Willie's, having become household names and worldwide stars. Country radio was now paying attention to acts half their age, but the irony wasn't lost on the band. In 2004, Rascal Flatts—then country radio's latest favorite band—had scored a No. 1 platinum single with "Bless the Broken Road," a song cowritten by Jeff Hanna that had appeared on one of the Dirt Band's earlier albums. Even though the Dirt Band's version hadn't been a hit, Jeff got the last laugh when he and his cowriters won a Grammy Award for the Best Country Song in 2005, thanks to the Rascal Flatts recording.

Their encore over, Jeff, John, Jimmie, and Bob rushed off the stage while the full house of 6,500 Canadian fans gave them a rousing ovation. As he bounded down the stairway on the side of the stage, John looked my way and said, "Follow me." We walked down the long corridor behind the bleachers and into the dressing room so he could put down his gear and catch his breath. A few minutes later, he turned to me again and said, "Let's go say 'hi' to Willie."

The Honeysuckle Rose IV was parked just outside the arena's rear entrance. The last bus of Willie's I'd been on was the Honeysuckle Rose II. It had gone into retirement, while—after many years of service to Willie—the Honeysuckle Rose III had eventually been given to his daughter, Paula, a touring singer like her dad. I knew about this latest incarnation of Willie's buses because I'd recently read that this one ran on biodiesel.

John knocked, and the Honeysuckle Rose IV door swung open. We went up the steps, waving to Willie's longtime driver, Gates "Gator" Moore, as we came aboard. And right there, in the "front room" of the bus, stood Red Headed Stranger himself, wearing a black T-shirt and jeans. Willie was all smiles as he said hello to John.

The Nitty Gritty Dirt Band—21st century line-up (L–R) Bob Carpenter, Jeff Hanna, Jimmie Fadden, and John McEuen.

Then John turned toward me and said, "Willie, I want you to meet my friend, Randy Poe. He's come up from LA to hang out with me for a few days."

Willie grinned, stuck out his hand, and said, "We've met before."

I was absolutely floored. The last time we had been in the same room was at

On the bus with Willie Nelson in Sydney, Nova Scotia, Canada.

Ray Charles's birthday party six years earlier. All I could muster was a mumbled, "Uh, yes, we have." I'd been ready for just about anything, but being recognized by Willie Nelson was not on the list.

John turned to Willie and said, "Why don't you play Randy your new song?" Willie moved over to his CD player and cued up the track "Whatever Happened To Peace On Earth?"—a politically charged song featuring Willie and several guest vocalists. I was shocked (or as close to shocked as I can get after more than three decades in the music business) by the strong lyrics questioning how much oil a human life is worth. As we stood there listening to the song, I couldn't help but notice that Willie had fired up a joint.

When the song ended, I looked at Willie and said, "You know how much trouble that song is going to get you into?"

Willie just smiled and said, "I was born for trouble."

I caught the reference and said, "*Born for Trouble*—that's the album that had 'Ain't Necessarily So' on it, right?"

Willie turned to John and said, "You've done brought me one of those guys who knows more about me than I do." Then he turned back to me, held out the joint, and said, "You wanna hit?"

In an instant, my mind flashed back to that moment in 1983 when this same man had asked me if it was okay to open his portion of the Songwriters Hall of Fame program with "Whiskey River." I took the joint between thumb and index finger, looked right into his eyes, and asked the same question I'd asked him twenty-three years earlier: "How could I possibly say no to Willie Nelson?"

★ ★ ★ ★ ★

During the intermission between the Dirt Band's set and Willie's, the Honeysuckle IV was *the* place to be. Willie's daughter Lana was there, so I was happy to finally have a chance to thank her in person for our email exchanges a few years earlier regarding "Kansas City."

When Willie's longtime drummer, Paul English, came on board, I asked John if he could take a photo of the two of us together. It turned out to be yet another shot of me with my mouth open. Apparently some lessons are never learned.

Although it was cool to spend some on-the-bus time with Willie, this was clearly not the right atmosphere for song plugging. Nobody five minutes away from going onstage to perform in front of thousands of people wants to be getting a sales pitch. So John and I thanked Willie for letting us come aboard, said goodbye to Paul, Lana, and the rest, and then headed back to the Dirt Band's dressing room.

"Me and Paul," or in this case, Paul and me. (I'm the one with his mouth open again.)

At this point in my career, when it comes to attending concerts, I've probably seen shows from backstage almost as many times as I've been an audience member out front. Most of the times I've been backstage, I've watched the opening act split for the hotel as soon as their set was over. When John and I walked into the dressing room after the visit to Willie's bus, I was surprised to see the rest of the NGDB members still there. As it turned out, for this tour Willie had asked the band to join him onstage during the gospel segment of his concert. So at precisely the same time each night, John, Jeff, Jimmie, and Bob would head from their dressing room to the side of the stage. Willie would then hail the band to come sing some gospel songs with him, and the audience would get to enjoy a second helping of the Dirt Band. From the audience members' perspective, it all appeared totally spontaneous. Ah, the beauty of showbiz.

I was glad to finally be back in my hotel room around midnight. It was four hours later in Nova Scotia than in LA, so to my brain and body, it felt like only eight o'clock p.m. I called home to check up on the family, checked all of my office emails for the day, responded to all of the urgent ones, chiseled

~TO PITCH OR~ NOT TO PITCH

I've occasionally pitched songs under much less than ideal conditions—and like most song pluggers in similar situations, I've come away with nothing to show for my efforts.

As every good poker player is well aware, you've got to know when to hold them, know when to fold them, and always keep an eye on the guy with the cards to make sure he isn't dealing from the bottom of the deck. But I digress . . .

The main thing you want to avoid is pitching a song at a bad time when there's a strong possibility you'll have a better chance the next day, the next week, or the next month.

Don't be like Will Ferrell in *Wedding Crashers*. (His character was the guy who went from trying to pick up women at weddings to hitting on women at funerals.) Just as there's a right time and a right place to pitch a tune, there are plenty of times and places that are just plain wrong.

With Willie only minutes away from hitting the stage, I knew better than to start telling him that I'd flown thousands of miles to play a song for him. Poodie Locke had already told me I was crazy. I didn't need to have his boss thinking the same thing.

When the question is to pitch or not to pitch, always let common sense be your guide.

away on the Duane Allman book for a while, and then tried to get some shuteye before the next day's ferry ride to Newfoundland. Unfortunately, the jet lag curse had me firmly in its grasp. By the time I finally drifted off to sleep, the sun was coming up in Nova Scotia. Ah, the beauty of showbiz . . .

CHAPTER FORTY-TWO

I woke up not so bright but extremely early on the morning of the 12th, checked out of the Cambridge Suites, and took a taxi to the port in North Sydney. Marine Atlantic's Caribou "super ferry" was docked in the harbor. I'd seen cruise ships in various Caribbean harbors, and I'd taken large boats from Long Beach to Catalina Island before, but I had never been on anything like this vessel. It was almost 600 feet long and over eighty feet wide. The massive back of the boat was open, allowing cars, trucks, and buses to enter. According to the brochure in the sparsely populated onshore waiting room, this beast could hold over 300 vehicles and 1,200 people.

At the appointed time, my fellow pedestrian travelers and I were led down to the Caribou's entrance. As I entered the five-story structure and stepped onto the escalator, I began to wonder if I would ever see John McEuen and the rest of the gang again. This thing was the size of a couple of football fields, with cabins and corridors everywhere.

I managed to find an information booth, but it was unoccupied. I was getting ready to search elsewhere for help when I noticed a sign on the wall, behind the empty booth, that said we would be entering a new time zone when we docked at Channel-Port aux Basques. I'd only learned about the (one-hour-later-than-Eastern) Atlantic Time Zone when I landed in Halifax two nights earlier. Now, according to the sign on the wall, I needed to set my watch forward another *half* hour thanks to something called the Newfoundland Time Zone. This whole trip had seemed a little weird from the start. With the half-hour time change coming, it was beginning to reach surreal proportions.

I walked past dozens of cabins that looked like miniature hotel rooms. Just as I was beginning to wonder if I was going to have to search every cabin on every floor of this monstrosity, I came to a section of the ferry that looked a lot like the waiting area of an airport terminal—an extremely large airport terminal. The room could seat hundreds of people, but there was practically nobody in the place. Apparently Fridays in May aren't a busy time for the Canadian ferry business.

Much to my relief, huddled together in a group next to one of the boat's gigantic windows overlooking the Cabot Strait were John, Mickey Raphael, Billy English, and Jody Payne. Sitting alone a few rows away from the others was Paul English, pen in hand, writing feverishly.

According to my brochure, the ferry ride over to Newfoundland was supposed to take anywhere from four and a half to six hours. As the minutes and hours slowly ticked away that day, I would come to discover that the brochure was hopelessly optimistic. But being the lucky guy that I am, the long slog across the Cabot Strait turned out to work in my favor—thanks primarily to the fact that by this time on the tour, everyone else in the Willie/NGDB cast and crew had been staring at each other for over two weeks. And there I sat—the "new guy."

Out of what I chalked up to sheer boredom, everybody seemed to want to talk to me. John introduced me to Billy and Jody. I knew that Billy English was probably related to Paul, since they both had the same last name. I had figured he was Paul's son, but Billy clarified for me that he was actually Paul's brother. (I was glad Paul was sitting far enough away from the rest of us that he couldn't hear my faux pas.) I learned from Jody Payne that he was living in Stapleton, Alabama, just a couple of towns over from Perdido—the tiny Alabama town I'd lived in as a child.

As the voyage and conversation continued, Mickey Raphael turned to me and said, "Tell me more about this Sinatra Song."

I was momentarily surprised that Mickey had remembered me telling Poodie and him why I had made the trip to Canada in the first place, until I realized my conversation with the two of them had taken place less than twenty-four hours earlier. It already felt like I'd been on the road for weeks instead of only two days.

On the ferry-boat heading toward Newfoundland, standing next to three very tall guys. (L–R) Me, John McEuen, Billy English, and Jody Payne.

"I can do better than tell you about it," I said. "I can play it for you." I reached into my bag, pulled out my iPod, and began to scroll through thousands of song titles. "Oh, look at this," I said. "I have your solo album on here too!"

What can I say? It pays to be a fan. Mickey wouldn't believe me until I handed the iPod over to him so he could see I'd downloaded all twelve tracks from his album *Hand to Mouth*. Then he handed it back to me so I could cue up "The Girls I Never Kissed."

We sat side by side in total silence as he listened to the Sinatra Song through the ear buds while I tried not to sweat like a hooker in church. When it ended, he smiled and asked, "Which one writes the music? Leiber or Stoller?"

"The Stoller half," I said.

"Man, I really dig those changes," he said. "Willie's a big Sinatra fan. You'll definitely have to play this for him."

I exhaled for the first time in about four minutes. "I'm glad you like it. Now it's just a matter of being able to get together with him long enough to play it for him."

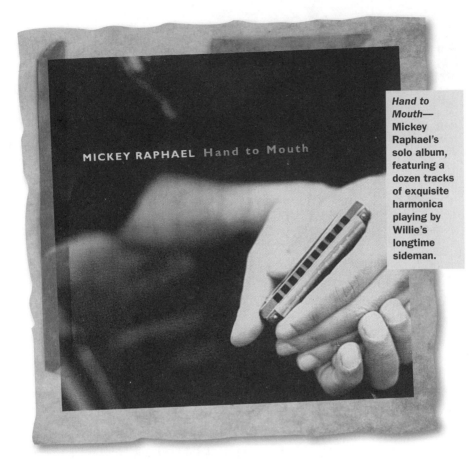

Hand to Mouth— Mickey Raphael's solo album, featuring a dozen tracks of exquisite harmonica playing by Willie's longtime sideman.

"You came this far," he told me. "I'm sure you'll find a way."

"From your mouth to Willie's ears," I said.

★ ★ ★ ★ ★

The Caribou felt like it was barely moving, which was actually the case. The brochure said the ferry's maximum speed was 22 knots—just over 25 miles per hour. The sea was choppy, and the wind must have been blowing in the wrong direction, because four and a half hours had passed, and all I could see in every direction was water. Mickey stood up and said, "Let's go for a stroll."

We went out onto the deck. It was May in Canada, which meant it was colder than the coldest day of winter in LA. I was beginning to think this wasn't such a great idea, until Mickey asked, "You wanna go see the bridge?"

When we arrived, the crew welcomed us in. As bridges go, this one made the one on the Starship Enterprise look like the dashboard of a 1965 Ford F-150 pickup truck. All of the men running the ship looked extremely competent, but the view out the massive windshield was more than a little unnerving to me. Mickey started asking them about the biggest waves they'd ever encountered between North Sydney and Channel-Port aux Basques, and their answers were starting to make me seasick. I found myself eager to get back down to the false safety of my seat a couple of stories below. If the big one was coming, I preferred not to know about it in advance.

As we were heading back to our seats, Mickey and I discussed one of Willie's then-recent albums called *Countryman*. It was a project that had begun in 1996, but thanks mainly to a shake-up at the label Willie was signed to at the time, it hadn't been released until late 2005. (The usual annual pink slips had been handed out, leaving everyone who supported the album on the hunt for new jobs and leaving *Countryman* languishing in the vault for nearly a decade.) Willie has made a lot of albums covering a lot of different genres over the years, but *Countryman* was his first and (so far) only foray into reggae. If most of the critics had their way, it was a place Willie wouldn't have forayed into in the first place. But I loved it. I was telling Mickey that my favorite track on the CD was the duet with Toots Hibbert, when we spotted one of Willie's road crew walking toward us. Mickey said, "Hey man, do you have any more of those *Countryman* guitar picks?" The roadie reached into his pocket and pulled out a small, white, triangular piece of plastic. "This is it," he said, "The last one."

"Let Randy have it," Mickey told him.

"Well, I don't want to take it if it's his last one," I said, lying through my teeth.

"No problem," the roadie said. "If there's one thing we've got plenty of, it's guitar picks. This is just the last of the *Countryman* batch. Enjoy."

I held the pick in the palm of my hand. On one side was an illustration of Willie with ponytails, wearing his usual red bandana. On the other side there was a bright green marijuana plant, with C-O-U-N-T-R-Y-M-A-N entwined

between the leaves. As guitar picks go, this one was pretty cool. I thanked the roadie and Mickey, and then stuffed it in my pocket. It wasn't exactly a St. Christopher medal, but I needed all the luck I could get on this trip.

Back inside the section of the boat we had now officially dubbed "The Terminal"— a bad pun based on a combination of the airportlike look of the place and the duration of the trip—I sat down next to John. We were over six hours into the four-and-a-half-hour trip when John started showing me photos of himself with Steve Martin, Jerry Garcia, and others. It was his Wall of Fame, laptop-style.

Just as it was beginning to feel like the fortieth day on Noah's ark, there was a noticeable stir of excitement in the room. Hearing a hushed murmur from the folks who weren't part of our immediate entourage, I looked up from John's computer and saw Willie strolling down the terminal aisle.

I would find out later that he'd been ensconced in the captain's quarters most of the trip. If the idea was to keep Willie away from the crowd, there'd been no need to bother. First of all, the small contingent of those traveling to Channel-Port aux Basques wasn't big enough to qualify as a crowd. Secondly, I had discovered over the last day and a half that Canadians are among the most polite people on the planet. There were no eBay-selling autograph seekers, no obnoxious loudmouths, no paparazzi stumbling all over each other—just friendly people, smiling at Willie as he walked by. A few shyly waved in his direction, and Willie waved back to each of them individually.

When Mickey spotted his longtime boss, he motioned for him to come over. Pointing at me, he said, "Randy's got a really rare Sinatra recording you need to hear."

"Really?" Willie asked, his ever-present smile growing even bigger.

I knew I had to think fast. I couldn't just hand him my iPod. Luckily, Willie was thinking even faster than I was. "Why don't you bring it to the bus while we're in Corner Brook? I'm a big Sinatra fan. I'd like to hear it."

"You got it," I said, trying not to leap out of my seat and give him a big hug.

Willie strolled on down the aisle, stopping to chat with Paul English. John looked up from his laptop and said, "See? Nothing to it."

Willie finished his conversation with Paul English and disappeared down the hall. As soon as Willie was gone, Paul took up his pen again and went back to work on whatever he'd been working on the entire trip.

★ ★ ★ ★ ★

Yesterday's Wine, Willie's eleventh album released during his long tenure on RCA, had come out in 1971. Like all the rest of his RCA recordings, it went virtually unnoticed at the time. In 1971, he was still four years away from signing with Columbia Records, the release of *Red Headed Stranger*, and genuine stardom. When *Yesterday's Wine* was finally released on CD for the first time in 1997, the critics raved—as well they should have. I'd bought the original vinyl release of the record back in the 1970s and was extremely impressed by what Willie had created—particularly the next to the last song on the album, "Me and Paul." It was the song with the line about Nashville being the roughest. The lyrics tell of the real-life trials and tribulations Willie Nelson and Paul English were going through while trying to survive during their early years in the world of country music. Clearly, they had both endured. They'd gotten the last laugh, and they were still laughing.

Yesterday's Wine—The album that included Willie's classic tales-of-the-road song, "Me and Paul."

I'd read a lot about Paul English over the years. I'd also seen a lot of photographs of him from his early days as Willie's drummer. In the photos, Paul wore more black than Johnny Cash attending a funeral. His wardrobe even included a black cape with a red satin lining. Combined with his black hat and his pointy jet-black goatee, Paul English looked like a Cowboy Satan sitting behind a drum kit. I could understand why Willie had put Paul in charge of collecting each night's pay. Who would dare refuse to give the devil his due?

But the Paul English I was looking at on the ferry ride to Newfoundland didn't look like anyone's vision of Satan. Wearing glasses—and with no black cowboy hat in sight—he looked a lot more like anyone's vision of granddad.

As I sat there trying not to stare at Willie's drummer, I thought back to a younger version of Paul English some twenty-three years earlier at the Songwriters Hall of Fame dinner in New York. Poodie might've made me a little nervous that night, but—intentionally or not—Paul English had appeared so menacing in those days that I never went within twenty-five feet of him.

He was the only person in Willie's band I'd yet to have a conversation with, so I took a deep breath and walked over to him. Since I'd gotten my picture taken with him the previous night on the bus, I figured there was a good chance he'd remember who I was. "What's that you've been working on this whole trip?" I asked.

He looked up at me and smiled. "Hey, son, have a seat right here and I'll show you."

I sat in the chair next to his and realized he was holding what looked like a book of crossword puzzles—but instead of words, he was writing numbers in the little squares.

"This is Sudoku," he said. "It's a Japanese numbers puzzle."

For the next few minutes, Paul went into excruciating detail explaining that Sudoku is made up of grids and subgrids. He told me that no subgrid could contain the same number twice. He showed me examples of games he'd already played, and then he showed me the one he was working on when I'd shown up. It didn't really matter. I had absolutely no clue what he was talking about. It certainly wasn't Paul's fault. I'm sure anyone who doesn't suffer from an inherent fear of numbers would've easily followed his explanation of how the game is played.

I was horrible at math in high school, and algebra was the one subject that almost prevented my graduation from college. The only time I can comprehend anything beyond basic math is when it's applied directly to music publishing. For example, I can tell you without blinking an eye that if a song has two copublishers, and if each copublisher owns 50 percent of the copyright, and if that same song has three cowriters who each wrote one third of the song, that means, in the case of mechanical royalties for every record sold or every audio file downloaded, the copublisher representing two of the writers would collect 58.333 percent, and the other copublisher representing the remaining writer would collect 41.666 percent. Trust me. I'm right.

As I listened to Paul's Sudoku instructions, my head was swimming. A few years later, I would learn that Sudoku actually has very little to do with math, but sitting next to Paul that day, all I knew was that numbers were involved. Then, to my great dismay, he pointed to a blank spot on one of the grids and asked me, "So, son, what number would go here?"

One of my many character flaws is an uncontrollable desire to please everybody. It pained me to have to let Paul know that he'd just spent the last five minutes trying to explain something that I had so utterly failed to grasp. I took a deep breath and went with my lucky number. "Three?" I asked.

"Why, son, you're a natural at this! I can't believe you got it right on your first try. Let me flip over a few pages to one of the harder puzzles and we'll have some real fun."

~ ENJOY THE VOYAGE ~

The main thing that keeps me drawn to the music business year after year is the mystery of never knowing what will happen next. What movie is in the pipeline that might be in need of a song from my catalog? What's the next TV show that's going to be music intensive? Who's getting ready to go into the studio? Who's going to be the "Next Big Thing?" And of course, whatever the answer to any of those questions might be, the next question is "How do I get my songs into the hands of the people who'll be making the decisions about what songs are going to be used?"

If you've ever tried to swim against a river's current, you know how difficult it can be. Sure, salmon do it, but once they finally reach their destination, they spawn and die. I always wondered why they didn't just do the whole thing in reverse—swim *downstream* and spawn. That way they wouldn't be nearly as exhausted. But I digress . . .

Song plugging often requires that you go with the flow. A few years ago, when television producer David E. Kelley requested to use a couple of Leiber and Stoller songs for his TV show *Ally McBeal*, I asked Helen Mallory (remember Helen from chapter 7?) to find out if it was just a coincidence or if Kelley was a Leiber and Stoller fan. After a little research, she told me she'd found out that he'd gone to see *Smokey Joe's Café: The Songs of Leiber & Stoller* on Broadway and loved it.

As soon as I found out that nugget of information, I had Helen send him the show's cast album and songbook. Then we sent him the two promotional CDs of Leiber and Stoller songs. After that, we sent him the six-CD boxed set of hits from all of our publishing catalogs.

During the five years the show ran, we ended up with over a dozen of our songs being used on *Ally McBeal*. When a soundtrack album from the show was released, we had three songs on that too. *Ally McBeal* is no longer with us except in reruns (which means we still receive performance royalties every time a show with one of our songs in it airs). Luckily though, David E. Kelley continues to produce new TV shows, and to this day, he's still using songs from the Leiber and Stoller catalog.

Some opportunities don't come by very often. But if someone likes your songs and wants more of the same, you might find yourself in for a nice long ride. If you do, be sure to enjoy the voyage.

I didn't know what to do. Since we were on a boat, running seemed a little silly, but it was the best option flashing through my mind. And then, at that very moment, a voice came over the loudspeakers announcing that the ferry was preparing to dock and that everyone should return to their seats.

Never mind that I was already seated. I'd been given my chance to escape, and I took it. I thanked him for his time and made a quick getaway back to the seat next to John's. In a matter of minutes, the Caribou had docked at Channel-Port aux Basques. Now all I had to do was find Tony the rental car man, and then be on my way to Corner Brook.

CHAPTER FORTY-THREE

When the Caribou docked at Channel-Port aux Basques, everyone in the touring entourage headed toward the band buses. As I stepped into the terminal, there stood Tony, sign in hand. He was clearly in a hurry. As soon as I told him I was the guy there for the rental car, he began to jabber away in his Prince Charles/Keith

Stalking the Red Headed Stranger

Richards/Bono accent. I caught something that sounded like "I'm late for my daughter's graduation," but it really could've been something about his lawyer's arbitration. I had no clue. He gave me a contract to sign, handed me a set of car keys, pointed to the parking lot, and was gone.

I walked out to the parking lot, located the rental, threw my luggage in the trunk, got in the car, started the engine—and then turned it back off. I sat there for a few moments, thinking to myself, "Where the hell am I and how the hell do I get to Corner Brook from here?" I had no GPS. I had no map. I had watched Willie's bus roll out of the belly of the Caribou, but it didn't cross my mind to watch which way it was heading. I was used to going to the Alamo counter at the airport and getting a map and detailed directions from someone who spoke something akin to American English. Tony had been in such a hurry he hadn't even had time to ask me if I wanted the extra insurance.

I got out of the car and walked back into the terminal. I went up to the information desk and asked how to get to Corner Brook. A very polite man proceeded to give me what were, no doubt, very detailed and concise directions. Unfortunately, his accent made the rental car guy sound like Walter Cronkite. I smiled and asked him to repeat everything, but it was no use.

Luckily, the fates had followed me all the way to Channel-Port aux Basques. A young man standing directly behind me said, "I'm buying a ticket for tomorrow's ferry. As soon as I'm done here, you can follow me to Highway 1. That's the road to Corner Brook."

"You must be from Nova Scotia," I said.

"Yes, I am. How did you know?" he asked.

"Because I actually understood every word you said."

★ ★ ★ ★ ★

I hopped back in the rental car and followed my new acquaintance's pickup truck through the streets of Channel-Port aux Basques. When we reached Highway 1, he pointed the direction I should go. I waved goodbye to yet another in a series of polite Canadians and began driving through some of the most incredible scenery I'd ever laid eyes on. To my right were massive red pines. To my left

~KNOW WHERE YOU'RE GOING~

Everyone who has ever been in a car with me is well aware that I have absolutely no sense of direction whatsoever. I can't deny it—without a GPS I probably wouldn't be able to find my own backyard. But despite my pitiful navigational skills, I always make it a point to know where I'm going.

If you've never had a song recorded, placed in a movie or a TV show, performed on a stage, or used in any other way, you're still at the starting gate. On the surface, that might seem like a negative. In reality, at least you know exactly where you are. You don't even have to ask "Where do I go from here?" You already know that the only direction to go from your current location is forward.

You can move forward by following some of the ideas I've expressed throughout this book. It took me years to develop a strategy that worked for me. Hopefully, some of my advice will be helpful and save you some time.

So let's address the elephant in the room. If you're a songwriter, you're not going anywhere without great songs. How do you know if your songs are good enough to make the trip? You have to let others hear them. I'm not talking about your mother. She thinks everything you do is great. I'm also not talking about your friends. They're all just impressed by the fact that you write songs in the first place. And I'm not talking about the other guys and gals in some songwriting club you belong to in Your Town Here. I'm sure they're all wonderful people, but unless they've already had success as songwriters themselves, they're not going to be much help to you in the advice department.

The way to know if your songs have what it takes to help you move forward is to play them for the people who matter—people already in the music business. That's why I've continually emphasized that you should get to know everyone in the music business you can. They're the people who can either help you or give you the unfortunate news you might be better off considering songwriting a hobby rather than a career. And the reason you need to meet everyone you can is because one person's opinion shouldn't be considered gospel. I've known plenty of songwriters who struggled a long time before they finally broke through.

So let's keep things positive. Let's say you get one of your songs used in a TV show. Now you've left home and made it to the end of the block. What's your next move? The answer is, you're going to keep moving forward. Use the fact you've gotten a song into that TV show for all it's worth. Remember all of those people you've been meeting in the music business? Don't be shy. Make sure they know you're not just a wannabe anymore. Turn one use into two—and then keep going.

Unless you have remarkable success right out of the gate, songwriting will probably have to be a part-time job. If you're like most songwriters, your goal is for it to become your career. The only way that's going to happen is for you to either act as your own song plugger or have someone who acts on your behalf. To have someone pitching your tunes generally means signing a deal with a music publisher. But even if you become so successful that music publishers start offering to throw money your way, that doesn't mean that you should take your foot off the accelerator and let someone else take the wheel. Some of the best songwriters I know have been responsible for getting their own songs recorded. Know where you're going.

was the Gulf of St. Lawrence. The view was so unbelievable that I had a difficult time keeping my eyes on the road. My bad driving didn't really matter all that much though, since there were very few other vehicles going either direction on Highway 1.

After several miles, I came over the top of a hill and saw the Honeysuckle Rose IV directly in front of me. A wiser person would have stayed behind Willie's bus all the way to Corner Brook. After all, if I was going to play the Sinatra Song for Willie, knowing where to find his bus might be helpful. But I've never been known for my slow driving, so I passed the bus and drove through more gorgeous scenery for another two hours, finally arriving at the Glynmill Inn just as the sun was setting.

While everyone else was enjoying a night off, I sat in my hotel room responding to more emails, returning phone calls, and working on the Allman bio. When I finally went to bed around midnight, the whole room began to rock back and forth, back and forth. After spending most of the day on the Caribou, the sensation of being on the ferry refused to leave me. For the first time, I finally understood what Willie meant when he sang "Still Is Still Moving to Me."

CHAPTER FORTY-FOUR

I woke up at ten o'clock the next morning, knowing this was the last possible day I'd have a chance to play the Sinatra Song for Willie. The following day, the whole entourage would be heading to Saint John's, a city on the opposite coast of Newfoundland. Willie and the Dirt Band were booked to play the first of two nights at Mile One Stadium in Saint John's the same day I was booked to return the rental car; catch the ferry back to Sydney, Nova Scotia; and start winging my way back to Los Angeles. It was literally now or never—and I didn't even want to consider the possibility of returning to LA without having accomplished the mission at hand.

I called John. He told me to meet him in the lobby of the hotel at noon. After a quick shower, I got dressed, put the CD and lyric sheet of the Sinatra Song in my bag, and—having nothing else to do but sit around and wonder if we were going to be able to find Willie's bus somewhere in Corner Brook—I ventured downstairs. I took a peak in the hotel restaurant and spotted Jeff Hanna, Jimmie Fadden, and Bob Carpenter having breakfast together. Bob saw me and waved me over to their table.

As I pulled up a chair, Bob's first words to me were, "Are you the Randy Poe who's a mathematician?"

Before I could answer, Jeff laughed and said, "Bob's been researching you on the Internet."

"No," I told them. "I'm not the mathematician. I'm also not the Randy Poe who's a real estate agent in Florida or the one who's the superintendent of schools in Kentucky. Thanks to the Internet, I've come across at least a dozen other people named Randy Poe."

The Nitty Gritty Dirt Band's Bob Carpenter, glowing behind the keyboards.

"Well then," Bob said, "Are you the Randy Poe whose email starts with the prefix 'bongorandy?'"

"You know, I never realized how much free time you have when you're on the road," I said. "Things must have gotten pretty boring for you to be googling me. But to answer your question, yes, I confess. I am bongorandy."

Jimmie suddenly perked up. "You like bongos?" he asked.

"Yep," I said. "I probably shouldn't admit this, but I've actually got an embarrassingly large collection of old vinyl by Preston Epps, Jack Castanzo, the Incredible Bongo Band, and a bunch of other players from the '50s and '60s."

"I collect bongos," Jimmie said.

At that moment, Bob and Jeff simultaneously slid their chairs back, rose from the table, gave me a quick wave, and disappeared out the restaurant door. After all those decades of the band being together, they both knew what was coming.

As it turns out, when it comes to bongo drums, Jimmie Fadden is a walking encyclopedia. In this case, he was a sitting encyclopedia, so I sat there with him and soaked it all in. I had found a kindred bongo spirit, and could have talked to Jimmie until show time—but just before noon, I saw John walk into the room.

I apologized to Jimmie for having to split, and I sincerely meant it. Since the time I was fifteen years old, I'd been a huge fan of the whole band, and now I had to walk away in the middle of a conversation with one of the heroes of my youth. Ironically, I was leaving him to go with another hero of my youth to search for Willie Nelson. It was turning into a pretty interesting day.

John and I headed for the rental car. "The first thing we have to do is find tonight's venue," John said.

"Do you have an address?" I asked him.

"No, but it shouldn't be too hard to find."

"So we're just going to drive around Corner Brook, Newfoundland, until we find the place?"

"Yep."

I drove to the end of the hotel's long driveway, looked at John, and asked, "Left or right?"

"Your guess is as good as mine," he said.

I turned right, drove for a while, turned right again at the next major inter-

Harpin'
Jimmie
Fadden—
Bongo
connoisseur
extraordi-
naire.

section, and sure enough, there at the top of a hill in the distance was another
hockey rink. "That's it," said John. "Just drive around to the back."

I drove through the parking lot and around toward the rear entrance of the
Pepsi Centre, where we encountered a barricade across the road with a "Do Not
Enter" sign on it. "Uh oh. What do we do now?" I said.

"We wait."

Sure enough, in a matter of seconds, a security guard came walking toward
us with a quizzical look on his face. John raised both hands, high enough for
the guard to see, and began playing air guitar. The security guard nodded in the
affirmative and moved the barricade out of the way. I looked at John and said,
"What the hell was that?"

"That's the international sign for 'I'm in the band.' It works for me every
time, anywhere in the world."

I drove around to the loading dock. We strolled into the hockey rink and went to the production office. It looked exactly like the production office did at the last venue. One of the women in the production office gave me my backstage pass, answered John's question about which hotel Willie's bus was parked at, and then told us where the catering room was. She hardly had to bother, because it was in the same spot the catering room had been at the hockey rink in Sydney. As we walked toward catering, we passed the dressing rooms and Willie's tuning room, which looked just like they had in Sydney.

"Wait a minute," I said to John. "Everything's exactly the same as it was two nights ago. After a while, how do you remember where you are?"

"Well, sometimes you don't."

"Seriously, is anything ever different?"

"Sure. We've played larger places, smaller places, outdoor festivals—every kind of venue you can imagine, we've played 'em. But the main difference is the audience. You never know how they're going to respond. It's the reaction of the crowd that always keeps it exciting."

We went into the catering room, grabbed a couple of cups of coffee, and then went to take a look at the hockey rink they'd be playing in that night. As we stood next to the stage, I saw Poodie and the soundman, Bobby Lemons, in the middle of the room, standing over the mixing console. As I walked toward them, Poodie shouted, "Did you play that song for Willie yet?"

"Not yet," I told him, "But today's the day."

He looked at me and grinned. "You really are crazy, you know that?"

"After that seven-hour ferry ride, there's no longer any doubt in my mind," I said.

I handed Bobby my disposable camera, looked at Poodie, and said, "Can I get my picture taken with you?"

"Sure," he said.

He threw one of his bearlike arms around my shoulder and smiled for the camera.

Bobby took the picture and handed the camera back to me. I thanked them both—and as I walked away, Poodie couldn't help himself. He pointed that famous index finger at me and shouted loud enough for everyone in the room to hear him:

"There are no bad days."—Poodie Locke

"That man's crazy!" I looked back and waved. He was grinning from ear to ear.

John and I headed back to the car. We knew the name of the hotel where Willie's bus was parked, but of course we had no clue where it was—so I just drove.

While John kept a lookout for the bus, we went around in circles for a while—thanks primarily to my lack of any sense of direction. When I realized I had passed the same building for the third time, I decided to drive toward the outskirts of town. Finally, John said, "There it is." And there it was. Willie's bus was parked next to a diner that was next to the hotel that he'd probably never set foot in the whole time he was in Corner Brook. The bus was his home.

By this point, I had no idea where we were in relation to our own hotel, but it didn't really matter to me at the moment. I just knew we had closed in on our target. I was all ready to go knock on the door of the bus when John said, "Let's eat!"

We walked into the diner, immediately spotting Jody Payne sitting at the counter. As we were saying hello to Willie's longtime guitar player, one of the waitresses shouted for us to sit anywhere. I looked toward the booths next to the window, and there, eating breakfast together, were Bobbie Nelson and Willie's daughter Lana.

A waitress brought us menus and coffee. A few moments later, a second waitress came over with a piece of paper and a pen. She looked at John shyly and asked, "Can I have your autograph?"

As John was signing the piece of paper, out of the corner of my eye I saw Bobbie and Lana heading our way. Lana said, "When you two get done with breakfast, come on over to the bus."

At this point, it was all beginning to feel like the world's longest (and most elaborate and most surreal) episode of *Candid Camera*. Surely I was being punked.

We ordered our breakfast, and then John began telling me another tale of the road. But all I could think about was Hunter Thompson's famous quote: "It never got weird enough for me." As my plate of scrambled eggs and other things I'm not allowed to eat was put in front of me, I thought to myself, "As of right now, it has definitely gotten weird enough for me."

~ TODAY'S THE DAY ~

Mel Fisher was a treasure hunter. In the late 1960s, he learned about a sunken Spanish galleon called the Nuestra Señora de Atocha. According to historical records, the Atocha had sunk somewhere off the coast of Key West, Florida, with a vast treasure on board. When Fisher began searching for the Atocha, he started each morning with the announcement to his crew, "Today's the day."

In 1971, after two years of searching, the Atocha's anchor was discovered. It appeared the treasure was only days away from being located. A short time later, a gold chain was found—another indication that Mel and his crew appeared to be closing in on the mother lode. Unbelievably, another two years would pass before Mel's son Kane would finally discover a single silver bar. Then, on July 13, 1975, Mel's son Dirk located five bronze canons from the ship. All indications were the treasure was practically in their grasp. But it was not to be.

Mel Fisher continued his search for ten more years before finally hitting the mother lode on July 20, 1985. He didn't give up after a year or two, or ten or fifteen. Every single morning for more than sixteen years, Mel Fisher confidently announced to his crew, "Today's the day."

Mel Fisher had the perfect song plugger attitude. When you're trying to pitch a song, the odds are almost always stacked against you. The competition is always fierce. The logistics involved in trying to get a specific song into the hands of a specific artist can be absolutely overwhelming. The best song pluggers have the same attitude Mel Fisher always had: "Today's the day."

CHAPTER FORTY-FIVE

★ ☆ ★

Breakfast had been eaten, the tab had been paid, and the time had come. John and I left the diner and walked over to the bus. Gator Moore opened the door before we could even knock. When John and I walked in, Willie was in his usual spot at the kitchen table. It was the same kitchen table (or an exact replica of the one) where Willie and my best friend Roger had passed that bottle of Jack Daniel's back and forth all those years ago.

As soon as he saw me, Willie stood up and said, "Oh hey! You got that Sinatra song for me to hear?"

For the last eight days, I had spent virtually every waking moment trying to figure out how I was going to find a way to get Willie Nelson to let me play the Sinatra Song for him. Incredibly, now that the task was at hand, *he* was the one asking *me* to let him hear it.

I handed Willie the CD and the lyric sheet. He put the CD in the player and then sat back down at the kitchen table. John sat on the sofa that ran parallel to the wall behind the driver's seat. I sat on the one that ran parallel to the wall behind the bus door. And so there we were—Willie Nelson, John McEuen, Lana Nelson, Gator Moore, Frank Sinatra, and me. Frank sang his heart out for all of us.

> *The old wolf sniffs the summer breeze*
> *And dreams about his youth*
> *For the sight of skirts above the knees*
> *Turns his hard-boiled brain to cheese*

And the scent of honey in the trees
Whets an old sweet tooth

The pretty girls go strolling by
I look at them and heave a sigh
And think of all the things I've missed
And all the pretty girls I never kissed

They smile from fields of daffodils
They wave from high and windy hills
In secret places by the sea
The girls I never kissed still wait for me

All the girls whose names I can't recall
Their faces haunt me still
All the pretty girls I never kissed
And never will

The girls of spring, the girls of fall
The girls of summer most of all
If only time did not exist
If only I could catch that boat I always missed
I'd go back and kiss
All the pretty girls I never kissed

As the last note faded away, Willie smiled. "Frank Sinatra is my favorite singer," he said. "And I read in a couple of interviews that he said I was his favorite. I've always been real proud of that."

"As well you should be," I said.

It was impossible for me to judge Willie's reaction to the song. He hadn't said, "I love it!" On the other hand, he didn't say anything negative either. What he did say was, "Tell me more about Leiber and Stoller."

I knew he must have heard about my bosses. Most people in the music business have. When the show *Smokey Joe's Café: The Songs of Leiber & Stoller* became a smash hit on Broadway, even much of the general public became aware of their names. In fact, back at Ray Charles's seventieth birthday party, Willie had met Mike Stoller in the Green Room. Maybe when he said "Tell me more about Leiber and Stoller," he'd just meant "How are they doing?" But I was so used to having to rattle off their list of hits for the uninitiated, I did the same for Willie. As I began telling him the songs they'd written and the records they'd produced, Willie fired up a joint that would've made Bob Marley nervous. When I told him they wrote "Kansas City," he said, "Hey, I cut that one!" Then he strolled over to the sofa and handed me the joint. What could I do? I took a hit and passed it back to him, and then continued listing Jerry and Mike's hits. When I got to "Hound Dog," Willie said, "I sure remember that one! Big Mama Thornton." Then he handed me the joint again.

I laughed and said, "Oh man, I can't wait to tell the guys that you know the original version of 'Hound Dog.' Most people think Elvis recorded it first, but Big Mama had an R&B hit with it three years before Elvis's record—and she actually got all of the words right."

Being the perfect hostess, Lana offered us coffee. I said I'd love a cup, and John said, "No thanks." I told Lana that John always said no to everything, and I always said yes to everything. It was a totally innocuous statement, but for some reason it seemed absolutely hysterical. When Willie passed the joint to me a third time, I began to realize the situation at hand: Willie's Daytime Pot was *way* more powerful than his Extra Lite Pre-Gig Pot. The joint he'd passed to me a couple of nights earlier had had no effect on me at all. The joint he was now passing my way for the fourth time had begun to cause visions of sugar plum fairies to dance in my head.

Willie began talking about Sinatra again, while I began to focus hard on just remaining conscious. The Sinatra Song had been played, and Willie had given it his undivided attention. For the moment, there was nothing more for me to do except find a way to make a graceful exit. The follow-up with others in Willie's camp would take place after I returned to LA. Right now, I just wanted to return to Planet Earth.

Meanwhile, John—who had also just heard the Sinatra Song for the first

(L-R) Me, Willie, and the joint I definitely should not have inhaled.

time—clearly liked it. I was relieved that he had dug the tune and was happy to have him as my coplugger.

I was just about to suggest that John and I hit the road, when Willie started talking about the next album his label wanted him to record. He told us it was supposed to be a collection of classic No. 1 country hits. Then he pulled out a big binder and said, "I've got this huge list of songs to choose from." At that point, he got up from the kitchen table, sat down next to John, and opened the binder. Then he looked at me, sitting opposite the two of them, and patted the space on the sofa next to him. I knew he meant for me to come sit next to the two of them so the three of us could look through the binder together—I just wasn't entirely sure if I could get from my sofa to his sofa. To my surprise, I felt light as a feather as I stood up, took a couple of steps forward, and then sat down next to Willie.

The first page of the binder was a list of No. 1 country hits from 1948. One of the songs on page one was "Deck of Cards." I pointed to the title and said, "T. Texas Tyler did that one." The song is actually a spoken-word piece about a group

~THE FOLLOW-THROUGH~

Just like pitching a baseball, pitching a song requires follow-through. The first move is to match the song with a specific artist. The second move is to establish a way to get the song to that artist (or the appropriate representative in that artist's camp). The third move is to make sure the song gets heard. The fourth move is to follow through.

Use the phone. Use email. Get a follow-up meeting if possible, but don't go overboard. If you do, you're not likely to be able to pitch another song to that artist in the future. Think of it as asking someone out on a date. If you try several times with no luck, it just might be time to stop asking.

Unless you're Irving Berlin (in which case you'd be well over 100 years old and quite dead), the vast majority of time the ultimate response to your pitch will be "The artist doesn't feel she's right for the song"—which is the music business equivalent of that classic break-up line, "It's not you. It's me."

Remember that book I was writing about Duane Allman? When it was published in hardback in the fall of 2006, it sold a whole lot of copies, and it's continuing to sell lots of copies in the paperback edition all these years later. When *Skydog: The Duane Allman Story* came out, I did book signings in LA, New York, and plenty of other places. National magazines, major newspapers, and major-market radio stations in the US, Canada, and literally around the world conducted interviews with me. Ninety-nine percent of the reviews the book received were absolute raves. For the longest time after the book came out, it was difficult for me to enjoy the book's success because of that other 1 percent—the tiny handful of negative reviews.

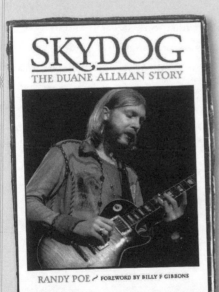

The point is this: I can tell you that you should never take rejection personally, but I know that my telling you won't make it so. Even if you don't want to take it personally (just like I didn't want to take those bad reviews personally), sometimes it's just impossible not to do so. The only way to get your songs recorded, or in a TV show or a movie, or in any other manner that songs are used, is to just keep on pitching. Once you have that first taste of success, the sting of all those earlier rejections might stay with you for a while, but eventually they will fade—just like the memory of that person from your past who once pulled that old line, "It's not you. It's me."

of soldiers in church. As all of the other soldiers pull out their prayer books, one soldier pulls out a deck of cards. The sergeant sees the soldier "playing cards" in church and has him taken to jail. When the Provost Marshall asks the soldier for an explanation, the soldier tells him what each of the cards in the deck symbolize to him (the 10 being the Ten Commandments, the Jack being the devil, the Queen being the Virgin Mary, and so forth). Willie—who understandably seemed surprised that I knew about a T. Texas Tyler record from 1948—turned to me, looked me right in the eye, and doing a perfect T. Texas Tyler impersonation, recited the last line of the song: "I was that soldier."

Sitting on a bus in a parking lot somewhere in Corner Brook, Newfoundland, Willie Nelson was, indeed, that soldier. He had spent decades on a crazy, mine-filled battlefield called the music business. Over the course of nearly half a century, he'd suffered numerous trials and tribulations, setbacks and defeats—his only weapons a guitar named Trigger, his voice, his songs, and his determination. When the smoke had cleared and the war was finally over, Willie Nelson was still standing—Trigger still at the ready.

Most men his age have already been retired for a decade or more. When asked about his own retirement plans, Willie has always given the same response: "All I do is play music and golf. Which one do you want me to give up?"

But perhaps the truth is that the road is more addictive than any drug. Once it's in the blood, it can't be given up. Old singers never die—they just ride away.

CHAPTER FORTY-SIX

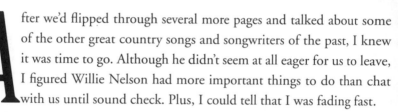

After we'd flipped through several more pages and talked about some of the other great country songs and songwriters of the past, I knew it was time to go. Although he didn't seem at all eager for us to leave, I figured Willie Nelson had more important things to do than chat with us until sound check. Plus, I could tell that I was fading fast.

It seemed like John and I had been on Willie's bus for well over an hour. It might've been two. It might have been ten minutes, but the powerful effects of Willie Weed suddenly made it feel like we'd been there for a week. In fact, it felt like I'd been awake for a week. My brain abruptly started spinning—clockwise for a while, and then counterclockwise for a while. I needed a bed—badly. I had no idea what time it was—except that I knew it was time to go.

My assignment had been to play the Sinatra Song for my buddy Willie in person, "face-to-face", and I had done exactly that. Whether or not he would ever record the song was anybody's guess, but as I sat on the sofa listening to John and Willie chatting with each other as if there was absolutely nothing wrong, I had just enough cognitive power left to know that John and I were going to have to leave immediately or I was going to have to curl up on the floor and pass out for several days—and I was absolutely positive that curling up on the floor and passing out would not appear at all professional on my part.

I looked at my watch, which refused to come into focus. The minute hand seemed to be spinning around forward, and the hour hand appeared to be spinning backward. The second hand didn't look like it was moving at all.

It was half past high-as-a-kite o'clock—*definitely* time to go. What the hell had Willie put in that joint?

I looked at John and said, "Hey man, I hate to say it, but we've got to get going."

"Already?" he asked.

"I'm afraid so. I've got to get back to the hotel and check in with the office."

Never mind the fact that it was a Saturday. It was the best excuse I could come up with under the circumstances. I felt myself involuntarily giving John the vigorous head nod—the very same one my friend from Nashville had given me when it was time for us to leave Willie's bus after the concert in Cerritos six years earlier.

The only problem I faced now was having to stand up—again. I watched John stand up. He seemed to have no problem with the concept at all. It was as if he didn't even have to think about it.

Willie was standing up too, as were Lana and Gator. That left just me. My feet were already on the floor, so that part of the equation was taken care of. Unfortunately, my ass seemed to be sitting in several gallons of molasses. I pressed both of my palms down firmly on the sofa and forced myself up with every ounce of strength in my body. The weed and gravity fought me hard, but victory was mine.

A wave of relief washed over me as I found myself in an upright position. I had been fully expecting to either fall flat on my face or go flying the entire width of the bus. Now all I had to do was walk to the door, go down a couple of steps, walk to the car, and then drive back to the hotel. How hard could that be?

Willie followed us outside, stood by the bus door, thanked us for coming to see him, and then turned to me, looked directly into my eyes, and thanked me for bringing him the Sinatra Song. Even in my near-catatonic state, I realized at that moment that Willie Nelson—one of the greatest singer/songwriter/guitarists ever to grace the planet—was also about the most polite and gracious person I'd ever met.

As we walked toward the car, John started telling me how amazed he was that I'd been able to smoke Willie's pot and not appear to be affected by it. Then he shared a story about a roadie he'd known who'd taken a couple of tokes off one of Willie's joints and immediately crawled into a corner and fallen asleep. I laughed—not too loudly, I hoped—and then climbed into the driver's seat of the rental car.

Of course, a sane human being would've tossed John the keys and said, "You'd better drive because I'm so completely whacked out of my gourd that I don't even know which pedal is the accelerator." Unfortunately, pride can be a terrible thing. On the other hand, if I hadn't been too proud to admit to Jerry Leiber that Willie Nelson and I weren't buddies, I never would've made the trip to Canada in the first place. I'd heard the phrase "pride and circumstance" all of my life. At that moment, I finally understood the concept.

I tried not to look too proud when I managed to successfully put the key in the ignition. Turning the key and starting the car was such a major accomplishment that I figured driving back to our hotel couldn't be all that difficult. There was only one problem—I had no clue where the hotel was. My survival instincts were just cognizant enough to sense that driving in circles all over Corner Brook in my condition would be a really bad idea.

As I sat there, getting ready to shift into drive, my mind flashed back to the only other time I'd ever been as high as I was at that moment. Not surprisingly, I'd been in Amsterdam. Also not surprisingly, the bar of the hotel I was staying in had a framed photo of Willie Nelson prominently displayed on the wall.

A lawyer friend of mine who shall remain nameless for obvious reasons was staying at another Amsterdam hotel a couple of miles away. He met me at a coffee shop that had come highly recommended by a local business associate. Once inside, I purchased a chunk of hash based primarily on its festive name: Christmas Pollen. It was a very brisk January evening as we sat in the coffee shop, lighting up this powerful chunk of hash the size of my thumb. We both had to fly to Nice, France, the next morning, which meant the hash had to be smoked that night. And smoke it we did. Needless to say, this was not among the more brilliant things I'd ever done.

When we exited the establishment a few hours later, it was snowing. We were chatting as we strolled along, watching the flakes falling harder and harder, rapidly covering the streets and sidewalks. After we had been walking slowly and talking even slower for about fifteen minutes, I stopped dead in my tracks.

"Where are we going?" I asked my friend.

"Well, I don't know where you're going, but I'm walking back to my hotel."

"But where's *my* hotel?"

"I have no idea," he said. "Look, all you have to do is walk back to the coffee shop and then retrace your steps from there back to your hotel."

"That sounds great in theory," I told him, "But we've made so many turns since we left that I don't even know how to get back to the coffee shop, no less my hotel."

"You could take a taxi."

I looked around. There wasn't a taxi in sight. In fact, there wasn't a car in sight. The snow was piling up fast.

"Not to worry," I said. "I'm sure I can find my way back."

After we said goodnight, I stood and watched as my friend shuffled down the sidewalk through the snow and disappeared around a corner. I had no idea what I was going to do.

For some reason, I closed my eyes and envisioned the outline of my hotel. It was being remodeled, so I envisioned everything about the exterior of the hotel—even the scaffolding. And then I started walking. With each passing block, I had no idea if I was walking toward the hotel or further away. But as I got to each corner, I looked down, closed my eyes, envisioned the outline of my hotel, opened my eyes again, and walked another block.

As previously noted, I have absolutely no sense of direction. But that night, barely capable of thinking at all, I discovered that my sense of direction kicks in only if I'm higher than Peter Pan tap-dancing on the Spire of Dublin. After less than a half hour of walking, I once again came to a corner, looked down, closed my eyes, and envisioned the outline of my hotel. When I opened my eyes and looked up, I was still seeing the outline of my hotel. There it was—the actual building, scaffolding and all—right in front of me.

★ ★ ★ ★ ★

From the time John McEuen and I had left our hotel a few hours earlier, we'd first gone to check out that night's venue, and then we'd journeyed all over

Corner Brook in search of Willie's bus. Now that we were back in the car, I revved the engine to stall for time while my addled brain formulated one of those typical pot-induced thoughts: our hotel could be in any direction, with the possible exceptions of straight up or straight down.

I decided visualizing our hotel was as good as any other strategy at that point, so I closed my eyes, drew the hotel's outline on the inside of my eyelids, shifted the rental car into drive, and hit the accelerator. Five minutes later, I pulled into the hotel parking lot.

"Wow!" John said. "That was amazing. I had no idea where the hotel was, but you drove straight to it."

I might've driven straight to it—but I sure as hell hadn't driven to it straight.

CHAPTER FORTY-SEVEN

As we headed back into the Glynmill Inn, John asked me to meet him in the lobby at four o'clock. I didn't dare look at my watch again, but when I got to my room, the digital clock on my nightstand said it was two thirty. I had an hour and a half to pull myself together.

I sat on my bed and opened my laptop to check my email. Between the usual junk and spam, there was a message from my old friend Joe von Herrmann. Joe had emailed to say he'd called my house, and that my wife had told him I was in Canada meeting with Willie Nelson. "Whatever you do," his message concluded, "Don't smoke Willie's pot!"

I sent back a two-word reply: "Too late."

I dragged myself into the bathroom for my second shower of the day. As soon as the hot water hit me, something went very wrong. Instead of sobering me up, it had the opposite effect. Suddenly I was ridiculously high again. All I could do was grab the showerhead and hang on. There was an entire carnival going on in my brain: roller coasters, Tilt-A-Whirls, cotton candy, juggling clowns with giant feet, carnies with bad teeth—all vying for my attention. When the paint started splashing onto the spin-art canvas, I knew I was in trouble. Standing up was no longer an option. I carefully let go of the showerhead—one hand at a time—and slowly sunk down.

As I lay there, my mind floated back to that day in Cerritos when I'd been on Willie's bus for the very first time. I'd been with my writer friend from Nashville. After we'd left the bus that afternoon, we'd gotten into my car, and my friend had mentioned something about an added ingredient in Willie's pot. I fought through the fog in my brain to try to recall what he'd said. Suddenly one of the big-shoed juggling clowns reappeared in front of me. In a cartoonish voice, he warbled, "Your writer friend from Nashville told you that he'd heard Willie's pot has dried psilocybin mushrooms in it."

"Dried mushrooms! Is that really true?" I asked.

The clown stopped juggling and looked me right in the eye. "You're asking me? How should I know? I'm just a figment of your altered consciousness."

The clown began to juggle again. I watched the balls as they flew higher and higher into the air. As I was looking up, one of the balls began coming back down, heading straight toward me at a very high rate of speed. Then I heard the cartoonish clown voice warble, "Oops!"

Suddenly, just like that moment in a Mickey Spillane novel when the butt of the gun comes down on the back of Mike Hammer's head, everything went black.

When I came to, the water had turned ice cold. My normal reaction would've been to leap out of the bathtub. Unfortunately, nothing normal had happened for me since I'd made the mistake of taking that first hit from Willie's joint a few hours earlier. I felt like I was swimming in quicksand. The only solution was to grab the side of the tub and roll myself out onto the floor. If there'd been anyone around to see me, it would've been the most embarrassing moment of my life.

Once I was finally on my feet and mobile again, I checked the clock on the nightstand. It was three fifty-five. I dried off, got dressed as fast as I could, and took the stairs two at a time down to the lobby. John and his banjo were already there. We hopped in the rental car and reenacted everything from earlier that day: I drove to the venue and pulled up to the blockade; John did his air guitar thing for the security guard again; I pulled into the exact same spot I'd parked in before—and then I checked the time. It was exactly four twenty. Even though I was no longer high, my watch continued to taunt me.

★ ★ ★ ★ ★

During sound check I stood in the middle of the near-empty arena as the Nitty Gritty Dirt Band played "Stand By Me." Thirty-six years earlier, this same band had been the first act I'd ever seen in person. Now they were playing a song that my bosses had written with Ben E. King—and they were playing it just for me.

As the music washed over the lucky few of us in the room that afternoon, I decided Poodie was wrong when he'd said I was crazy. I would've been crazy *not* to have made this trip. But he was absolutely right about one thing: "There are no bad days."

CHAPTER FORTY-EIGHT

The show at the Pepsi Centre in Corner Brook started at seven thirty-five p.m.—and from the opening chord, the Nitty Gritty Dirt Band was on fire. The crowd reaction was much more enthusiastic than it had been in Sydney. Watching the Pepsi Centre audience cheering and singing along confirmed what John had told me earlier that day: even though the venues might frequently look the same, it's the reaction of

(L–R) Jeff Hanna, Jimmie Fadden, me, and John McEuen on the night of the band's fortieth anniversary.

the fans that make every show different. But on this evening, something very special was in the air. I didn't realize what it was until Jeff Hanna announced between songs that this very night—May 13th, 2006—was the band's fortieth anniversary. The audience erupted. I cheered too. Everybody wants to be a part of history—and that night, we all were.

The guys finished their encore by out-springing Springsteen with a country-rocking version of "Cadillac Ranch," leaving several thousand Canadians scream-ing for more. I stood by the side of the stage as the members of the Dirt Band came running down the steps, each one sweat-soaked and grinning from ear to ear. Jimmie Fadden grabbed me as he went by, and the five of us quickly headed down the empty corridor toward the dressing room. I heard a voice in the distance and glanced over my shoulder. Poodie was standing behind us at the hallway entrance next to the stage. He was waving his arms and shouting that the band had to come back for another encore. The crowd was still cheering so loudly that we could barely hear him. All eyes turned to Jeff. He just smiled, shook his head, and kept walking toward the dressing room. I looked at him in disbelief—and then he hit me with the oldest, truest, most perfect show-biz cliché of them all: "Always leave 'em wanting more."

Jeff Hanna—
"Always
leave 'em
wanting
more."

ACKNOWLEDGMENTS

★ ✷ ★

Thank you to the following: Jerry Leiber, Mike Stoller, Willie Nelson, and the Nitty Gritty Dirt Band: Jeff Hanna, John McEuen, Jimmie Fadden, and Bob Carpenter. Special thanks to Peter Stoller, Jeff Hanna, and Mickey Raphael for reading the manuscript and making suggestions and corrections; to Tom Russell & Sylvia Tyson for their wonderful book, *And Then I Wrote: The Songwriter Speaks*; to Sam Teicher for always being there with his camera when I needed him; to April Anderson and Linda Moran of the Songwriters Hall of Fame; and to all of the people at Hal Leonard Books who were involved in every facet of the creation of this one: Mike Edison, editor extraordinaire; Marybeth Keating, project editor; Joanna Dalin, copy editor; Doerte Fischen-Rath, cover designer; and Damien Castaneda, interior designer. Thanks, as always, to Roger Deitz for his ear and his advice. Also, I want to recognize the good folks who were a part of the Leiber & Stoller organization back when we wuz young: Helen Mallory, Dennis O'Donnell, Ed Arrow, Brian Rawlings, Joan Schulman, Connie Ambrosch-Ashton, the late Teressa Rowell, Phyllis Rosenberg, Lisa Phelps, Laurie Leitzel, Ken Buchanan, Astrid Karyn Kristy, Thalia Saposhnik Karny, Royd Haston, Eric Higginbottom, Mark McCutchen, Marissa Levyns Bennett, Lesley Wright, Kelly Townsend, Monikka Stallworth, David Quan, Pinki Marsolek, and Marilyn Levy.

And finally, a very, very special thanks to my wife, Mina, for absolutely everything.

★ ★ ★ ★ ★

SUPPORT FARM AID

INDEX

★ ☆ ★

I N D E X